MOROCCO

Also by Shirley Kay

The Arab World
Digging Into the Past
The Egyptians
The Bedouin
Travels in Saudi Arabia
Saudi Arabia

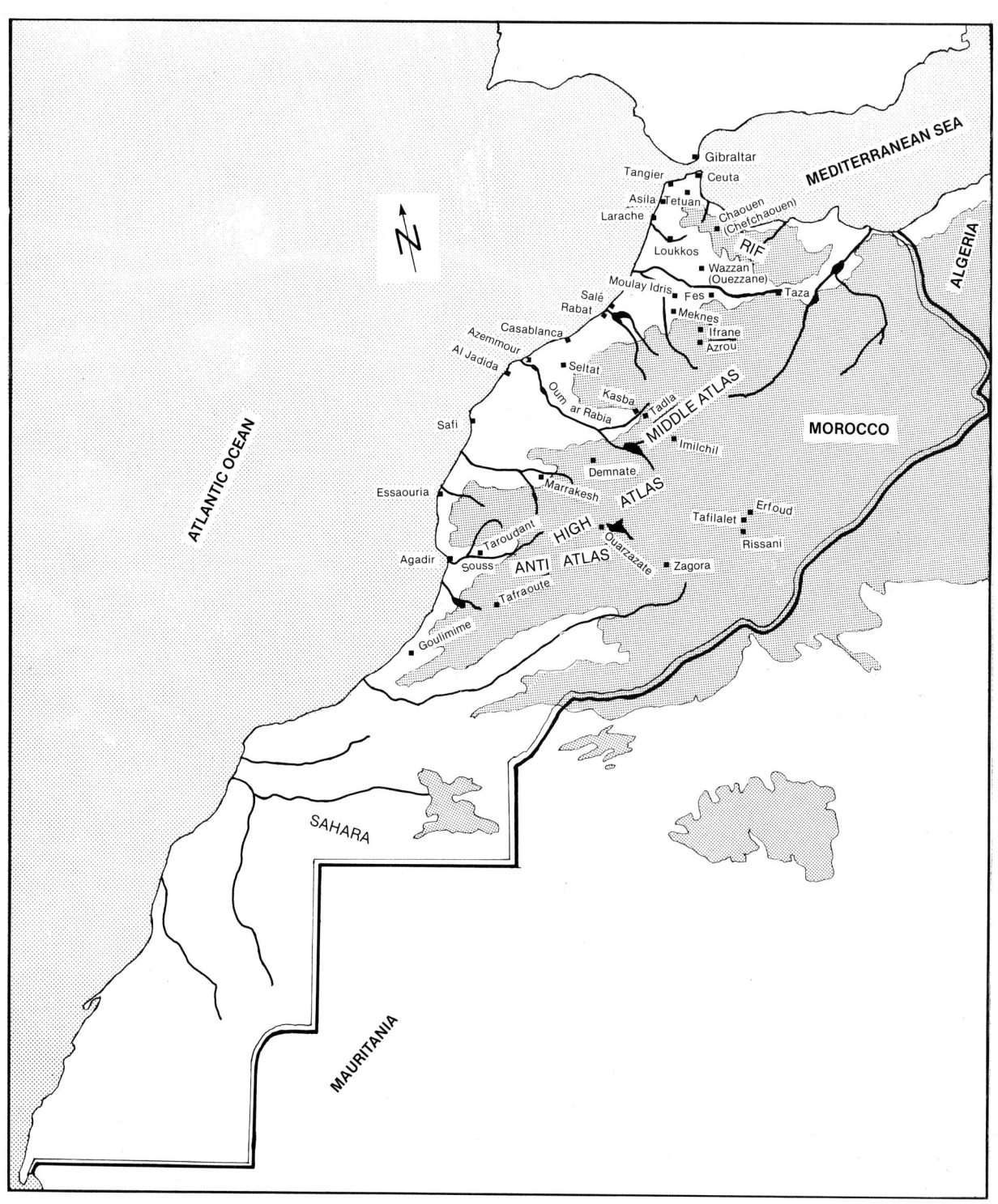

MOROCCO

Shirley Kay

Namara Publications

First published by Namara Publications Limited 1980
Namara House
45/46 Poland Street, London W1

Copyright © 1980 by Shirley Kay

ISBN 0 7043 2224 2

Typeset by BSC Typesetting Ltd, London
Printed and bound by
Shenval '80', Harlow, Essex.

For Tim, Gigi, Berny, Katy, Toby and Jean Luc –
who all loved Morocco too and shared many of my
wanderings there.

I should like to thank the Office National Maroccain de Tourisme for providing some of the black-and-white photographs used in the book. I also thank the following friends who lent me their books or photographs (many of which were ancient and particularly precious to them): M. Hassan Guessous, Canon Cecil Greene, M. Guy Martinet, M. Nils Nilsson, M. Jean Luc Soler, M. Gerard del Vecchio, and Mrs Kerry Jane Vacher and the Mamounia Hotel.

Contents

Introduction

'There are more books written on Barbary (Morocco) than on any other country, and yet there is no country with which we are so little acquainted,' remarked a British consul in Marrakesh some 200 years ago. His words still hold good today for most of the books about Morocco published in this century have been written in French. They have encouraged me to write this book in the hope of illustrating, for English-speaking readers, something of the life of the people, and in the hope of evoking the colourful past which lies behind their golden city walls. In the last century, and before, English travellers were fascinated by Morocco and a number of them made their homes there. I have drawn on their books to show the Morocco of olden times.

I have not tried to write a comprehensive guide book for there are already many good ones from which to choose. Most complete and authoritative is the *Guide Bleu* which exists in an English version, the *Blue Guide* to Morocco. Original English guide books include the *Travellers' Guide to Morocco,* 1972, by Christopher Kininmouth, the *Complete Guide to Morocco,* 1974, by Jane Holliday, and the *Fodor's Morocco,* 1977. If you intend to travel in remoter districts it pays to obtain the most recent guide book available since the road and hotel networks are being expanded constantly. If your taste is for things of long ago then the first guide book of them all, Leo Africanus's *The History and Description of Africa* (first published in 1526), should be your companion.

The spelling of Moroccan names has, I fear, quite defeated me. I can only seek refuge behind D. H. Lawrence's oft quoted comment, in the preface to his *Seven Pillars of Wisdom:* 'Arabic names won't go into English, exactly, for their consonants are not the same as ours, and their vowels, like ours, vary from district to district . . . I spell my names anyhow, to show what rot the systems are.' The problems are compounded when the names are half Berber in the first place, and all have been processed through French as through some great mincing machine. Lawrence, had he visited Morocco, would have delighted in the local potential for inconsistency. On the road to the Rif, for example, successive signposts point towards Chechaouene, Chaouen, Chefchaouen (all one town) and they could have added Xauen, Chauen, Shawan, Chaouene and so on.

I have used common English transliterations for well-known words such as Tangier, Muhammad, *al* (the definite article), but have kept to the French system for other names which you might not, otherwise, find on a map. *Oued,* a river valley, should rightly be *wad* in English; the French use 'ou' for our 'w', 'dj' for our 'j', 'e' for our 'a' (*el* not *al* for 'the'). I have taken another liberty, too: that of simply adding an 's' to an Arabic word to make it plural, a system quite unknown to the Arabs for whom the plural of *jinn*, 'genie', for instance, is *junun*. To save explaining the meaning of a word twice over I have merely written *jinns, funduqs* and many other, quite unreal, English versions.

9

Applauding the dancers (ONMT)

1 Arabs and Berbers

From the Bay of Algeciras on Spain's southern shore two rocky promontories can be seen rising from the sea. That which is close to hand is the Rock of Gibraltar; the other, further off across a short stretch of turbulent sea, is the headland of Ceuta. Known to the ancient Greeks as the Pillars of Hercules these rocks guard the Straits of Gibraltar at their narrowest point. It is but an hour's crossing by ferry from one side to the other.

In this hour, however, the traveller moves from one world to another, from christian Europe to muslim Africa, to the land of Morocco which is exotically, excitingly different from the countries which he has left behind to the north. True, the historical links between the peoples on either side of these narrow waters have been intimately close: Algeciras and Gibraltar on the north side are Arab names, dating back to the times when the Moors of Morocco ruled all of southern Spain, while Ceuta on the southern shore is a Spanish corruption of an Arabic name for, thanks to similar historical accidents, Spain rules the enclave of Ceuta, just as Britain rules the Rock of Gibraltar. Both towns are separated by frontiers from their hinterland; each strikes a foreign note.

This briefest of crossings is a foretaste of the complex historical threads which have gone to make up the Kingdom of Morocco and its people. For, although Morocco, in Arabic, is known as the Land of the Furthest West, yet it has always been as much of a crossroads as a journey's end. Its people have come from Arabia to the east, from Africa to the south, from Spain to the north: the blood of Berbers, Arabs, neg-roes and Europeans runs in their veins and shows in their faces. It would be hard to define a typical Moroccan though perhaps the Mediterranean look of brown eyes, olive skin and black hair is indeed the most common.

The streets of the towns are thronged with gently moving, gaily chattering crowds gazing into the tiny, open-fronted shops of the *medinas* (old towns – *medina* is the Arabic word for town), or the large glass-fronted stores in the modern streets. Moroccans rarely run; even to hurry is considered somewhat undignified. 'Never run when you can walk, never walk when you can stand, never stand when you can sit', runs a Moroccan proverb. And in the suburbs of the towns and the countryside this is precisely what they do, for most of them seem to get about sitting comfortably atop the paniers on the back of a donkey or mule.

The crowds in the streets and sitting at pavement cafés consist predominantly of men; the visitor from Europe often asks, 'But where are all the women?', for they seem strangely few and far between. Yet to the visitor from Arabia the women are oddly noticeable for, in a traditional muslim country, the woman's place is still considered to be in the home and Moroccan women are increasingly coming out into the world. True, in the towns, the older women are still veiled, covering the lower part of their faces with a little triangle of material which many now allow to slip down off their noses so only the lips are hidden. But the girls and young women rarely hide their faces and, in most country districts and the mountains, both young and old go unveiled.

In the past, veiling was considered the smart thing to do, it was the fashion of the town, differentiating the stylish city lady, who cared about preserving her fair complexion, from her country bumpkin cousin. Country women who had never veiled often began to do so when they moved into the town to live. Even visiting English women found there were advantages to the custom. Lady Agnes Grove, who was adventurous enough to spend *Seventy One Days Camping in Morocco* in 1901, noted in her book that she wore an opaque veil for the journey. She had taken seriously the advice of a friend who said, 'Look at Mrs. A., she went out there young and pretty, and returned in two months, burnt up and damaged beyond repair, all for want of a little precaution. Be advised and wear a non-transparent veil.' It was a world away from the promises of today's travel agents whose brochures advertise permanent sunshine and a glorious suntan as the rewards of a trip to Morocco.

Moroccan women's traditional dress is also being abandoned gradually in the towns. Older women may still wear long dresses covered by the *haik,* a piece of cloth draped over their heads and, in the strictest areas, arranged so as to cover all but one eye, or the fashionable *kaftan,* a long tailored robe with matching hood, slit up to the knee on either side, and produced in a wide range of bright colours. But the schoolgirls and young secretaries and shop assistants wear short skirts or trousers, while those who are half-way there wear a short dress under their *kaftan* and the hood thrown back. Groups of friends walk along arm in arm, dressed in the complete range from high western fashion to full Islamic veiling. On the beach at Rabat I watched two friends dressed in smartly matching black, only for one it was a black *kaftan* and veil and for her friend a black bikini.

The women often appear, at first sight, hump-backed but the bulge on their back is invariably a baby, buried (if small) under an all-covering blanket, peering eagerly around or

Berber girl at Imilchil

asleep, its head lolling against the back of its mother's neck, if older.

Like their women, the men are increasingly adopting European wear, especially in the towns. But they usually crown their western outfit with a little woollen or crocheted cap, often in the brightest of colours. Their traditional *jellaba,* woven in warm wool in brown, or white, or grey, is such a practical garment, especially in winter, that it is still worn by most men, even over their European trousers. Their heads are usually swathed in a white turban and some of the older men wear the red *tarbush,* or Turkish-style *fez.* In bad weather the peaked hood of the *jellaba* is drawn up; through the rain or mist they look like a colony of medieval monks.

12

Preparing for a mountain wedding (ONMT)

Yet looks are deceptive: a small boy from the depths of his cowl, surrounded by his sheep in a satisfyingly biblical tableau, may startle you with his fluent command of French, Spanish, English or German. The Moroccans are great linguists and have been willing to adapt over the years to a variety of languages which they tackle with supreme confidence. Perhaps about half the population grows up speaking Berber; at school they learn Arabic and, throughout most of the country, French as well. In the north the majority speak Spanish while on the tourist routes they will try their tongue at any language which may sell their goods. 'You come inside, just for looking,' a merchant in the *souq* urges; 'I am not guide, I am student; I go with you to practise my English, no money,' a youth in the city insists, but you will end up in his uncle's carpet shop just the same. On the High Atlas a little Berber boy offers his geodes and amethysts in German; he is crestfallen when we refuse them in English but perks up when he finds a chance to bargain in French after all.

This need to make contact with the foreign visitor, the source of ready money, drives even the smallest of children to acquire fluency in a language they have never been taught. For in Morocco, where the population is increasing with frightening speed, even the children must learn to fend for themselves, to contribute to the family income. In the fifteenth century, it is estimated, there were less than 6 million people; at the turn of this century there were still estimated to be some 6 million Moroccans; in the 1936 census there were just under 6 million; by 1960 11.6 million; today there are over 19 million and, by 1985, it is expected that there will be at least 23 million.

In the past the population was reduced once in every twenty-five years or so by periodic famines which swept the land after the rains had failed, and by the plagues which invariably followed. Tribal warfare shortened the life-span of men, while a nomadic or semi-nomadic existence took its toll of the babies. None of the peoples who made up the population were spared. The Berbers of the mountains, the Arabs of the plains and the cities, the negroes who lived with both and were the descendants of slaves, and the Jews who lived apart in both country and town, all were cut down periodically by famine and plague as they had been from the time when their ancestors first came to the land.

When this time was, for the Berbers, is one of the more intriguing mysteries of Morocco and one that has greatly taxed scholars this century past. The mystery appealed, even in the eighteenth century, to Englishmen such as John Windus who travelled to Meknes in 1721. He wrote of the Berber language that it was 'supposed to be the ancient Punick or Carthaginian, which, I think, would greatly deserve being particularly enquired into'.

When the Romans came to North Africa they found the Berbers in possession of the land and called them barbarians (from which our name for them derives). They spoke no recognizable language and indeed, even today, few affinities between their language and that of other peoples have been found. It seems to be most closely related to the language of the Copts which, in turn, derives from ancient Egyptian. One theory for their origins, therefore, is that they were the original inhabitants of the Sahara and when that region dried out and became desert they settled on its periphery, some going to the valley of the Nile, others establishing themselves along the coasts of North Africa and in the mountains of Algeria and Morocco.

Yet the Berbers are a fair-skinned people, not quite what one would expect for the inhabitants of the Sahara, even in the days when it was savannah. Today, despite the centuries of racial mixing, one still finds Berbers with blue eyes and fair or red hair, especially in the Rif mountains. Might they not, then, have come from the north? There are puzzling elements in their culture, however, which seem to come from the Middle East. Their mud-built *kasbahs* (fortified houses) on the edge of the desert might have moved straight from south-west Arabia, apart from those elements of their decoration which seem to have come from ancient Mesopotamia; while the little clay figurines which the Berber children of remote valleys still make convinced Walter Harris, the resident *Times* correspondent in Morocco at the turn of the century, that they must be descendants of the Phoenicians who made identical figures.

Until very recently they lived a warlike, tribal existence in their mountain fastnesses, fighting neighbouring tribes or, if these were not interested in battle, the men of the next village. Disputes still flare up with amazing speed in the streets and can lead to fisticuffs; but today's passers-by always struggle to separate the combatants rather than joining in the fray. Berber folklore sings of battles, murder and sudden death and showed them fearless and inured to pain. They had a saying about the peoples of North Africa that 'The Tunisian is a woman, the Algerian a man and the Moroccan a lion.' They were in the forefront of the Arab invasion of

Berber girls of the High Atlas

Spain in the eighth century (Gibraltar is named after the Berber leader who was first to land there, Jebel Tariq, 'Tariq's mountain'), and of Franco's repetition of it in 1936 when his Berber Rif troops formed the backbone of his forces.

They had a passion for freedom. The Berbers of the Rif call themselves *Imazighen,* which means 'freemen', and all would put up the toughest of fights to remain free. Yet when they saw that they must lose most of them were practical enough to accept defeat with the knowledge that it was the will of Allah, consoled by the old Berber saying: 'Kiss the hand that you cannot cut off.'

The Berbers have always lived a village life, governed in a democratic manner by representative councils with a member from each family group. The family is the basic element of their society and, although they became firm Muslims within a few centuries of the Arab invasion, very few Berber men take more than one wife: 'May the locusts devour the crops of the man with two wives,' the Berbers would say. Today only about half the population of Morocco speak Berber at home and consider themselves Berbers but, nevertheless, the vast majority of Moroccans must in fact be descended from Berber stock.

Yet Morocco today is an Arab nation and feels itself to be strongly a member of the Arab world; Arabic is the official language and Islam the religion of the state, even though Morocco is furthest of any Arab land from the original home of the Arabs and the number of Arab tribesmen who settled there in the past must have been quite small. The Arab invaders first arrived in the seventh century. An initial thrust reached Morocco in 648 AD and a more substantial invasion was led by Uqbah ibn Nafi in 670 AD. He reached the shores of the Atlantic and looked out to the west across the waves. There, it is said, he drove his horse into the sea until it almost lost its footing and cried out to God to witness that there was no more land in that direction for him to conquer.

15

Berber boys of the Middle Atlas

The Arabs, however, did not establish themselves permanently in Morocco until 788 AD. At that time Moulay Idris, a descendant of the Prophet (which the title *Moulay* denotes), fled from a battle in which he had been defeated near Mecca. He settled in the old Roman capital of Volubilis and was accepted as leader by the local Berber tribe. He extended his influence over the neighbouring districts and founded a small town at Fes. But in 791 he was poisoned by an emissary of the Caliph in the east, and buried at Moulay Idris, the purely Arab town on the hills above Volubilis. After his death a son, Moulay Idris II, was born to his Berber concubine. The boy was proclaimed ruler at the age of eleven. He founded another town at Fes (which is now the Andalus district), on the opposite bank of the river to that founded by his father. The town was destined to grow into the greatest city in Morocco and to serve for centuries as capital of the land.

The early Arabs settled as city folk and left the countryside to the Berbers but, in the eleventh century, Arab bedouin tribes began to arrive in considerable numbers. They were led by the turbulent tribe of the Beni Hilal who had been causing so much trouble in Egypt that the powerful Egyptian dynasty drove them westwards, hoping to kill two birds with one stone by ridding themselves of the troublesome bedouin and having them crush the equally troublesome regime in Tunisia. In Morocco the bedouin moved into the coastal plain where they continued a largely nomadic existence until the beginning of the present century; they wandered also in the deserts of the south.

Among the Arabs the most respected members of society were those (known as the *shurfa*), who could claim descent from the Prophet Muhammad himself. A *shereef* (in the singular) was believed to possess grace, *baraka,* and to be able to give a blessing to those who came to him

Mother and child

(Gerard del Vecchio)

Man and his donkey, Fes

Grandmother, Middle Atlas

Shepherd boy, Middle Atlas

Basket souq, Rabat

Carpet souq, Marrakesh

Silver Koran case

Koutoubia minaret, Marrakesh

Minaret made from Portuguese watch tower, Al Jadida

Chellah minaret, Rabat

Kasbah of Boulouane

Zellijs (mosaic tiles) and stucco wall decoration

Courtyard of a traditional town house

or merely touched the hem of his gown. The ordinary people were happy to support the *shurfa* in their midst for the sake of their blessing.

One of the strangest tales concerning a *shereef* involves an Englishwoman. In the past century the Grand Shereef of Wazzan, greatest of the Moroccan *shurfa* and accepted leader of much of northern Morocco, fell deeply in love with a young English girl, Emily Keene. She had accompanied an English family to Tangier which was becoming something of a winter resort. One day, riding down a mountainside in the country, her saddle slipped and her horse reared in fright on the steep precipitous track. Emily thought her last moment had come but, in that second, a voice said, 'All is well,' and a strong hand seized her bridle while its owner caught her as she fell. Hajj Abdesalam, Grand Shereef of Wazzan, fell too – head-over-heels in love with the girl he had saved.

They were married in 1873, on Emily's twenty-third birthday. At first they were idyllically happy but it was a very foreign relationship to implant in the heart of traditional Moroccan society and eventually the Grand Shereef became estranged from her. She suspected that he was being poisoned; he certainly began to drink heavily. But before his death in 1892 he named his English wife the inheritor of his *baraka* and the guardian of all his children, those of his previous marriages as well as Emily's own two sons.

So she was able to live on, happy and respected in Tangier which had become her home and where for many years she treated the sick, having been the first to introduce vaccination during a smallpox epidemic. She lived to a great old age, finally dying, aged ninety-two, in 1941, surrounded by her sons and numerous grandchildren and great-grandchildren.

Over the centuries entire Berber tribes became Arabized and adopted Arabic as their native tongue. Today many thousands of people are leaving the countryside to seek their fortunes in the city where they soon adopt Arabic, the language of town life.

While Berber and Arab tribesmen and townsmen may look so similar that it is difficult, if not impossible, for the uninitiated to tell them apart, there are among both of them large numbers of dark-skinned people, the descendants of slaves or concubines. Over the centuries the Arab caravans which crossed the Sahara from the oases south of the Atlas mountains would bring back, along with their cargoes of gold and ivory, trains of dark-skinned slaves. The good-looking slave girls were often taken as concubines or wives by the rich and powerful and their children grew up as full members of the Arab or Berber family to which they were born. Most of the leading families thus have dark-skinned as well as light-skinned members and

Dark-skinned girls in the Atlas

some of the country's most powerful men, such as Sultan Moulay Ismail, who built Meknes and ruled for fifty-five years, or Thami al Glaoui, Pasha of Marrakesh and uncrowned king of southern Morocco under the French, were sons of coloured mothers.

Of course many of those of coloured blood were not born into rich families and often found themselves doing the menial tasks, working as household servants and in heavy labour. Others were born into country families and worked the fields along with their lighter-skinned relatives.

A further important influx of people came to Morocco from the north. When the Arabic

kingdom of southern Spain finally fell to the christian princes of Castile and Aragon in 1492, nearly 800 years after it was first founded, the muslim inhabitants, known as Moriscos, were forced to flee. Many indeed had left long before for the Christians had been whittling away the Moorish domains for the past three centuries. Some opted to stay on in their beloved Andalusia but they, too, were finally expelled in 1609. In a fervour of religious intolerance the Spanish expelled the Jews along with the Muslims and both sought refuge in Morocco.

These refugees from Spain came from a highly developed, sophisticated society. They

A falconer at Marrakesh

of their hospitality and is usually the first thing offered to a visitor. The preparation of this tea involves a satisfying ritual which is carried out before the guest. Boiling water is poured onto green tea and mint in a tall metal (preferably silver or silver plated) teapot. Sugar is broken from a long conical block (the phallic-shaped parcels wrapped in blue paper in the grocers' shops turn out to be block sugar). A little tea is poured into a glass and tasted by the host, more sugar is added (it is always served very sweet), it is left to brew for a few more minutes, tasted again, another adjustment, then a little is poured into each of the handleless glasses on the tray and handed round to the guests. They pick up the glasses gingerly by the rim for it is difficult not to burn the fingers. The glasses will be filled again and again until the guests can drink no more. Mint tea is very refreshing especially if one can restrain one's host's passion for sugar.

In the houses of the wealthy mint tea may well be served in English teapots known as Richard Wrights. These silver teapots were manufactured in Manchester, in the latter part of the last century and the early years of this, especially for the Moroccan market. They were designed by the founder of the firm, Richard Wright, who had fallen in love with Morocco and spent many months in Fes where he was able to study the ritual of Moroccan tea making. Recently these much-loved teapots have been produced again, in Birmingham, and are once more appearing on Moroccan tables. Britain can claim another stake in the Moroccan tea ritual for it was British traders who sold tea to Morocco in the first place.

An invitation to eat in a wealthy Moroccan household is an invitation to a feast. Moroccans actively enjoy food; they have a delicious cuisine of their own to which they have added such French dishes as appeal to them. They take their duties as host seriously, feeling that the guest

brought skills and learning with them which made the cities of Morocco among the finest of their day. And they brought a heritage of light skin and fair hair for, among the Moriscos, were many descendants of converts from the original christian population of southern Spain. Fair-haired children are often seen playing in the streets of old Fes today.

Hospitality

Moroccans are extraordinarily friendly and hospitable and even the poorest of them will invite you into their cottage or tent if you show signs of being friendly too. Mint tea is the cornerstone

19

must rise from their table unable to eat another crumb.

Meals are usually served on low round tables with the guests sitting on the wide padded benches, which run along the walls of the room, or on low stools facing them. The dish of food is set in the middle of the table and each guest serves himself, traditionally eating with his fingers, now often using cutlery instead. Where fingers are used water will be poured over the guest's hands and soap and towel offered, before and after the meal. He must eat with his right hand only as in all muslim societies.

These formal meals consist of many courses, each of which is composed mainly of meat, though, near the sea, fish may be served as one course. The first course will probably be *pastilla*, an enormous round pie consisting of flaky pastry filled with pigeon, ground almonds and spices. It is a sweet-savoury dish for the top of the pie is strewn with icing sugar and cinnamon. Another course may be a *tagine*, the Moroccan stew which is cooked and served in a shallow brown pottery dish with a high matching conical lid. When the lid is removed a delicious smell of meat and spices emerges. The dish is cooked long and slowly and usually contains some form of fruit – prunes, quinces, apricots or raisins – or perhaps olives and almonds, cooked with the meat. The sauce is very rich and tasty and the spices prevent the *tagine* being over-sweet and sickly. (Two cookery books by Moroccan ladies — *Moroccan Cooking* by Latifa Bennani-Smires and *Secrets of Moroccan Cookery* by Fettouma Benkirane have recently been published in English versions and give the visitor a chance to try these dishes at home.)

There will probably be a chicken dish for Moroccans have some excellent chicken recipes. Favourites are chicken cooked with preserved lemons (which one sees in piles in the markets) or with almonds and olives. Young pigeons make another favourite dish and these are served stuffed with a mixture of raisins, nuts and spices, or covered with paper-thin pancakes.

When the guest feels he can eat no more he must still take something of each dish if it be only to dip his bread in the delicious sauce or to break off a small morsel of the meat.

The great dish for important meals is the *michoui*, a whole roast lamb served often on a bed of rice. Such lambs are often spit roasted and provide the centre-piece for the food at major festivals, such as the Eid al Kabir, or at wedding feasts.

No meal would be complete, however, without a plate of the Moroccan national dish, *couscous*. It is difficult to do justice to *couscous* in words; in practice I have never met anyone who did not like it. Thomas Pellow, who was taken captive in the eighteenth century and lived in Morocco for twenty-three years, wrote how he missed 'cuscassooe', which was 'actually very good, grateful and nourishing', and would have made it on his return home had he been able. The preparation, however, is long and difficult, involving the steaming of semolina over meat and vegetables and rolling it out to separate the large grains. It is served in a great pile with the meat and vegetables in a hollow on top, and is brought in covered with a conical rush cover. Experts can roll the grains into a neat ball with one hand and pop it into their mouths. Foreigners usually admit defeat and resort gratefully to a spoon or fork.

While *couscous* served with vegetables alone may well be part of the staple diet of the people, the other dishes described above are largely for entertaining, feast days, or the tables of the rich. Meat is expensive in Morocco but vegetables and fruit are cheap, plentiful, varied and superb. In the markets they are sold carefully arranged in artistic piles and displays, making them all the more tempting. Almost every vegetable and fruit that one has ever known grows somewhere in Morocco, at some season or other: oranges, lemons, tangerines and grapefruits are the staple fruits in winter and, with modern cultivation, one can have strawberries at Christmas: summer fruits include peaches, nectarines, figs, pomeg-

Old carpenter in Rissani market

ranates, apricots, grapes, and melons so cheap they are almost given away.

Arts and Crafts

The Moroccans have drawn on their rich blend of cultures and races, and on their fertile imagi-nation, to create a wide range of traditional arts and crafts which survive and are practised to this day. Some years ago craftwork was suffering a serious decline, as in many other countries where the hand-produced gave way to the industrially manufactured. As craftsmen left the countryside they abandoned their trade; many of the Jews who had been the leading jewellers left the country. Some crafts died out altogether.

However, positive government encouragement and the establishment of craft cooperatives where master craftsmen work and teach the young, and the growing market provided by the tourist industry, have revived craftwork. While mass production, in carpet factories for example, and of silver jewellery, may to some extent have lowered the quality, beautiful objects are still produced and there is a mass market of unusual attractive crafts at reasonable prices.

Most interesting for the tourist is a stroll around the streets of the old *medinas,* especially of Fes and Marrakesh, where you can watch the craftsmen at work. This work often requires great precision and a keen eye. Watch a leather worker making the incised and gilded decoration on a book cover or wallet, or a metal worker laying the incised silver scrolls onto his iron-work swans, stirrups or vases. Fingers and tools move rapidly in tiny booths with the poorest of lighting. Watch the small boys at work hammering the design into a brass tray or copper pot in some tunnel-like alley of Fes or Meknes. Each of these handcrafts is the product of immense labour.

The metal work is carried out with the simplest of tools, a charcoal fire in the back of the booth, a hammer and nail for incising the pattern. The metal *souqs* can be among the most colourful when the sunbeams glint through bamboo roofing on copper and brass displayed in incredible quantities for tourist and local consumption alike. Many of the pots and pans on sale are old and in other stalls boys are at work sanding them to a new and gleaming finish, soldering holes, knocking out dents. A glance at these old pots shows the styles from which modern kettles and saucepans have derived.

While the pots and pans are of a simple and pure design, silver work is usually ornate. One section of the *souq* will specialize in the silver

dishes, trays, teapots and conical covers which seem to be *de rigueur* as wedding gifts. They are covered with design and decoration and have a rather whitish gleam. Silver in Morocco is not hallmarked and is often mixed in part with other metals. It is not priced according to its purity, often not even according to the intricacy of the design, but simply by weight.

True gold coins are popular in headbands and necklaces and modern gold trinkets and bracelets glitter in the gold *souqs* of the big cities. But the sought-after, traditional Berber jewellery is of silver, or silver combined with the chunky, semi-precious stones so beloved by the tribesmen – yellow or orange amber, red coral, blue-green mazonite from the Sahara desert to the south. Necklaces of these stones with their glowing colours can be the most tempting of all, especially when they have been restrung by some clever jeweller to modern taste. The prices, however, are always high for the country people set great value on these stones.

One of the most attractive pieces of Moroccan jewellery is the *fibula,* an antique version of the safety-pin whose origin goes back to prehistoric times and which is still found in similar forms in the gaelic jewellery of Scotland. The basic form is a stout pin which passes through the cloth and is held in place by a crescent ring swivelled under the pin tip. Hanging from the ring, in the Moroccan version, are a variety of decorative pendants of which the grandest are the triangular cloak pins. These massive matching pins hold the cloak in place on each shoulder and are linked together with a silver chain. The large triangular ornaments are incised and often decorated with inlaid enamel in blue, green and yellow.

Jewellery often incorporates magical or tribal symbols. The Hand of Fatima, often in very stylized form, is one of the most popular designs for pendants. Creatures such as the tortoise and salamander also appear in jewellery. Similar symbols may form the basis of the design for rugs and blankets which are otherwise decorated

In the copper *souq* (ONMT)

with purely geometric patterns.

Weaving is an important and long-established craft in Morocco. The pastoral tribes, with their emphasis on rearing sheep and goats, had the wool necessary for weaving and the need for woven goods in the cold nights and winters of the Rif and Atlas mountains. They produced the smooth, woven black cloth of their tents which can still be seen today in the desert and oases south of the Atlas, in the Middle Atlas, and in the rich farmlands around Meknes where the tents often stand beside a permanent farmstead, a sign of their semi-nomadic use. Blankets and rugs, *hambels,* were also produced by the same

Potter's workshop, Safi

smooth-woven technique. They can be very attractive especially those based on stripes of cream, red and black. Recently in the *souq* old rugs of this kind have been cut up to make little waistcoats and jackets with a surprisingly fashionable look. The tribes also weave the warm *jellabas,* worn universally by the men in the countryside and mountains, and the striped hooded cloaks worn in winter by the women and girls of some mountain tribes.

Perhaps better known than the smooth-woven rugs are the Moroccan tufted rugs. Rug production has been greatly encouraged by the government and rugs are now an important export. These rugs are woven by women and young girls whose services are especially sought since they can knot the wool rapidly with their small neat fingers. The rug designs and colours used were particular to the different tribes, while

complex designs, based to some extent on Persian rugs, were produced in a few of the big cities such as Rabat. Rugs in the past were woven in the home by the women of the family; some still are today, though more and more in the towns the women and girls come in to work in carpet factories where the dyes used are artificial and the designs become stereotyped.

Here the girls sit in a row, six or eight to a bench, in front of the upright loom on which together they work their carpet. A team of girls can produce one square metre of carpet per day, knotting and cutting endlessly, in one quick, deft movement. They work long hours for low wages, but the end product, created with so much labour, is not cheap. Government prices for the various qualities of carpet are published and posted in the main carpet-buying centres. The government cooperatives also sell at official fixed prices.

In small remote towns the local carpets can be seen in the place where they are made and the colours vary with the dyes available and local custom: in Azrou in the Middle Atlas, for instance, the carpets are the natural-cream colour of the Middle Atlas tribes, with a brown geometric design in one corner, the symbol of the tribe; at Ouarzazate on the edge of the Sahara nearly all the carpets are a deep saffron colour; while at Chichaoua between Marrakesh and Essaouira the carpets, displayed in a charming old farmstead, are deep red. Old carpets can still be found, and their prices are no higher, perhaps even lower, than those of new carpets, but they are few and far between.

The painted woodwork, furniture and doorways are more commonly old than new. In old Moorish houses the doors, beams and sometimes entire ceilings were painted in geometric or floral patterns and often with fine workmanship. The colours were usually deep dull reds, greens, golds and deep blues. Furniture was relatively scant, consisting of wooden benches with coloured mattresses and cushions, but many houses boasted a painted wooden chest,

Potter at work

perhaps a painted tray with conical cover for serving food, and often delightful sets of painted shelves, each shelf supported on a row of little arches. Such relics can still be found in antique shops while modern versions of this painted furniture, done in brighter colours and often in green or turquoise, are made today, especially in Tetuan. Picture and mirror frames are typical of this modern production.

Colour too is the key to much of the pottery which is made throughout the Kingdom. The glazed pottery of the towns is decorated in brilliant colours with each town having its own particular styles and shades. Old pottery, of which some can still be found, especially in antique shops, has more muted colours, more gentle greens, blues and yellows, and commands a far higher price.

The potteries of Fes make the finest ware, decorated with highly complex, deep-blue line designs, always geometric. Safi potteries also have a great output; their bowls and dishes tend to be multi-coloured, on a white or cream background, but they have some fine turquoise products and vases and pottery drums with a monochrome pattern.

Leather work is another craft which has been highly developed by the Moors, both in Spain in the Middle Ages and throughout the centuries in Morocco. While leather is tanned, dyed and worked in many towns, Fes is undoubtedly the great centre of the industry and a visit to the tanneries there is not to be missed. Most widespread use for leather within the country is in the traditional men's footwear, the heel-less slippers known as *babouches*. These slippers are made in natural colours, in reds and oranges for children, but, above all, in a yellow pointed-toed version which is the most popular wear, especially for any kind of formal occasion. In the old *medinas* can be found rows upon rows of stalls selling only *babouches*.

The leather is worked also into belts and bags and cases of all kinds. Coloured skins are made up into wallets, desk sets, book and magazine

covers, and decorative caskets. Larger caskets are covered with natural-colour leather, making veritable seamen's trunks. Leather hats, waistcoats and leggings reflect local fashions as well as an attempt to interest the tourist.

A little surprisingly perhaps, for a strongly Islamic country, painting has become very popular in Morocco in recent years. Islam has the same prohibition on making graven images which is found in Christianity and Judaism, and this has been strictly interpreted over the years to include any representations of human and animal figures. The sculptures found in Morocco are Roman; traditional painting and architectural decoration is based on geometric or floral designs and inscriptions from the Koran.

There is now, however, a strong current of

Basket *souq*

naïve paintings. Most colourful figure in this school is the indomitable Chaibia Tallal with her flamboyant gipsy looks and powerful personality. She struggled for years as a young widowed mother to bring up her talented painter son, Hossein, and give him the training he sought. One day she took to dabbling with his paints and found the talent ran in the family. Today she is highly successful in her own right.

Her experience recalls a story told by Peter Mayne in *The Alleys of Marrakesh*. He was struggling to make ends meet and seized on the current vogue of getting one's servant to paint, to bring in a little income. Low and behold, his servant did have a knack of producing naïves but naïvely failed to grasp that the income was intended to be shared.

Muhammad ben Allal, one of today's leading painters, began life as a cook in a household in Marrakesh, fortunately the household of a painter. The painter encouraged his efforts and he began to produce enchanting scenes of Moroccan life, set against traditional backgrounds.

Perhaps Morocco's best-known painter is Hassan al Glaoui, also from Marrakesh but from the other end of the social scale for his father was the famous Pasha. Al Glaoui produces, above all, slightly stylized paintings of the traditional *Fantasias*, marked by horses with immensely long, slender legs. His paintings are often seen on posters advertising Morocco.

27

Defences of Essaouira

28

2 Barbary and the British

Morocco over the years has been known by a variety of names and so have her people. The earliest writers called the people 'Ethiopians', a name still used by foreigners up to the eighteenth century. The Romans called the country Mauritania Tingitana, the civilized part of it that is – civilized by them of course and centred on Tangier which they called Tingis. Today the name, Mauritania, seems to have worked its way southward and applies to the country to the south.

Beyond the Roman *limes* were the 'barbarian' tribes and the Romans' name for them stuck to the whole of the country for many centuries. As late as the eighteenth century it was known to the English as Western Barbary, feared for the Barbary corsairs who haunted its coasts.

The inhabitants of Barbary, however, were always referred to as the Moors, a name immortalized in English by *Othello,* the Moor of Venice. As late as the 1950s Moroccans were called Moors in English books, although I never hear anyone use the term today. The Moroccans, for their part, still call Christians *Roumi,* a distant memory of Roman times.

The country's present name comes from that of the city of the south, Marrakesh (pronounced Marāksh by its inhabitants), which was frequently the capital and always a power to be reckoned with. Its name began to be used for the country as a whole in the sixteenth century. Moroccans themselves call their land *Al Maghreb,* 'Land of the Setting Sun' or *Al Maghreb al Aksa,* 'Land of the Furthest West', to be more precise. For us, the term Maghreb implies all the north-west African states – Tunisia, Algeria and Morocco.

Morocco first appears in written history in the fifth century BC. A Carthaginian general, Hanno, was sent on a voyage of discovery along her coast and wrote a description of what he saw which included herds of elephants and other wild beasts at seaside lagoons. He founded a number of colonies there, to serve as trading posts, and the Carthaginians became firmly established. They traded by silent barter, piling their wares on the shore and withdrawing to their boats, while the natives placed gold beside the pile. When the Carthaginians were satisfied with the quantity of gold they took it, leaving their goods in exchange. In the Middle Ages Moroccan traders still dealt in exactly similar fashion with the negroes south of the Sahara. The Carthaginians told hair-raising tales of the lands beyond the Pillars of Hercules to keep out their rivals, the Greeks, who wove these tales into the legend of the labours of Hercules, supposedly sited on the Moroccan shore.

When Carthage fell to the Romans the Berber kingdoms of North Africa came under increasing Roman pressure. Juba II, King of Mauritania, was brought up in Rome as a hostage. While there he married Cleopatra Silene, daughter of the ill-fated match between Cleopatra and Mark Antony. They called their son Ptolemy. When he recovered his kingdom Juba ruled well and the land prospered. Agriculture flourished, cities were embellished like the Roman ones, his purple dye manufacture at Essaouira produced the highest quality of purple. A magnificent bronze bust of him, found at Volubilis, shows a sensitive, intelligent face. But the Emperor Caligula coveted the kingdom.

When young Ptolemy inherited the crown he was invited to the imperial games at Lyons; Caligula was incensed that Ptolemy's purple gown was finer than his own and seized the excuse to have him assassinated.

The Romans took the Berber state and developed Roman towns there, towns inhabited still by Berbers and notable for their art rather than their architecture. The mosaics, which floor the private houses of Volubilis, are a delight to visit; the collection of Roman bronzes found there are among the finest in the world.

During the Dark Ages of Europe the light of learning was shining in the Arab lands to the east and south. Universities were founded in the great Arab capitals; the Al Azhar university in Cairo is over a thousand years old. In southern Spain the universities of the Arab kingdoms of Al Andalus were the first to pay professors and so attracted the best brains of Europe and the east. In Morocco the university of Qarawiyin in Fes, founded eleven centuries ago, is claimed to be the oldest extant university in the world.

Spain had been conquered for Islam in 711, largely by the Berbers of North Africa. Soon they acquired a worthy ruler, the last of the Ummayad princes from Damascus, who alone had escaped the holocaust when the rest of his family were assassinated by a rival dynasty, the Abbasids. He brought with him a love of the sophisticated culture which had flourished in Damascus. But he was no artistic weakling; when his enemies sent out a governor to rule Spain he returned the unfortunate man's head to them, wrapped in a flag.

Spain became the most civilized country in Europe and its light shone strongly across the Straits to Morocco. When the military strength of Al Andalus weakened the Moroccans were there to send help and, sometimes, the helpers stayed to govern. The medieval Moroccan dynasties, desert tribes who, each in turn, conquered the settled lands to the north, were eager to learn from their sophisticated neighbours.

Roman ruins of Volubilis

The first of them, the Almoravids, who had built Marrakesh in the eleventh century to be their capital, introduced Hispano-Moorish architecture to Morocco, with the elegant *kubba* in the centre of Marrakesh, the bridge over the Oued Tensift north of the city and an extension of the Qarawiyin.

Their successors, the Almohads, religious ascetics who had descended on them from the mountain fastness of Tinmel, were conquerors and builders of even greater energy. Outstanding among them was Yakub al Mansur who pushed the Christians back to the north of Spain and built extensively, both in Al Andalus and in Morocco. His three great minarets, the Giralda of Seville, the Koutoubia of Marrakesh and the Tour Hassan of Rabat, are the most splendid of this period. The Almohads brought security and prosperity to Morocco: commerce and agricul-

Courtyard of a Roman house, Volubilis

ture flourished, sugar-cane was grown in the Souss and near Marrakesh and salt was traded weight for weight for gold. Chroniclers spoke of this 'land full of blessings'. But the Almohads needed troops for their campaigns in Spain. They invited the wild Arabian Beni Hilal tribe to Morocco; these nomads moved into the plains where agriculture was swept away before their grazing flocks. The Almohads continued to fortify their cities: the city walls of Marrakesh and Rabat and the monumental gateways of the Oudaias and Bab Rouah in Rabat were built.

The Merinids, who followed them, also fought the Christians in Spain and, at home, developed Moorish architecture at its most refined. They built many of the exquisite *medersas* (theological colleges) which are the pearls of the old Moroccan cities. These colleges have something of the character of Oxford and Cambridge colleges, with their students' rooms built around a central courtyard, but they are more compact and far more ornate.

Despite the efforts of succeeding Moroccan dynasties the fortunes of Islam in Spain over the centuries fared increasingly badly. The little christian city-states of the north managed at times to sink their rivalries long enough for a concerted attack. One by one the muslim city-states fell to them, first Toledo, then Cordoba, then Seville. Only Granada was left and there the civilization of Al Andalus survived for a further two and a half centuries until it too finally fell, in 1492, to the combined might of the Catholic Kings, Isabella of Castile and Ferdinand of Aragon.

The Moors were driven out of Spain after nearly 800 years, during which they had taken the southern part of the land to a high peak of civilization. But worse was to follow for their Moroccan allies: the Christians in their turn were now carried forward by a wave of religious fervour and imperial enthusiasm. Between 1415, when they seized Ceuta, and 1514, the Portuguese took and fortified most of the ports along the coast of Morocco. Their incursions led

Old Portuguese town of Al Jadida (Mazagan)

to the rise of yet another Moroccan dynasty, the Saadians, a tough desert tribe who were not afraid to fight the intruders for their homeland. By the end of the sixteenth century they had recovered all the ports except Ceuta, Tangier and Mazagan and had decisively defeated the

Portuguese at the Battle of the Three Kings. The tide of history was not, after all, to be reversed: there would be no christian state in Morocco as there had been a muslim one in Spain.

Yet the Saadians too were to enjoy only a century of power before another Arab tribe, the Alawi, came out of the desert to the south to found a dynasty which has continued to the present day and has lived through the profound changes which have brought Morocco from a medieval feudal land to a modern state.

J. B. delt.

Safi

The first British who visited Morocco have left but little account of themselves. A simple tablet found in Volubilis tells of a troop of legionaries recruited in England and stationed there in 190 A.D. It was a thousand years before others were to follow in their footsteps and leave an account of their experiences.

At that time, King John of England was finding his own people difficult to control. His barons did not like the way he had treated his brother, Richard the Lion Heart; in 1209 the Pope had excommunicated him and the French were threatening to invade. He was desperately in need of an ally and thought of the Almohad ruler, Muhammad al Nasir, in Marrakesh. He sent two knights accompanied by a clerk, Robert of London, who related how King John offered to become a Muslim and make his kingdom pay tribute in exchange for Moroccan support. The Emir Muhammad laughed at this: King John must be a man of little consequence if he would so lightly change his faith and put his lands in thrall. He dismissed the English messengers but, noticing as they left that the clerk was singularly ill-favoured with one arm longer than the other and deformed fingers, the Emir concluded that such a man must be particularly wise to have been chosen for such a mission.

He called him back and questioned him closely about his King and the state of his country. The clerk's answers in no way led him to change his decision to have nothing to do with King John. He gave Robert gifts which the latter presented to the King on his return. The King, in turn, gave Robert custody of St Alban's Abbey and thus his tale came to be recorded in the Abbey chronicles.

When the English again took an interest in Morocco it was their sweet tooth which drew them back. The Moroccans grew sugar-cane which could be traded for English cloth and armaments. In the 1550s British merchant vessels left London for Safi and Agadir, returning with cargoes of sugar, dates and almonds. A list of British imports from Morocco for the year 1574-5 gives, 'Refined sugar, 2068 chests (a chest contained 300 lbs), at a value of £20,680; unrefined sugar, 585 hogsheads for £3,873; molasses, 217 tons for £2,170; suckettes, 1400 lbs for £64; 600 lbs of marmalade for £20, along with such articles as goatskins, ostrich feathers, almonds, aniseed and dates, together amounting to less than £1600.'

Sugar was a luxury commodity reserved for the rich. Queen Elizabeth's household ordered sixty chests of Moroccan sugar in 1589; the British royal family, it is said, would have no other than Moroccan sugar on its tables until well into the last century. They were not the only ones eager to trade for this commodity: the Italians were already exchanging marble for sugar, on a weight for weight basis, which accounts for the fine marble floors in many Moroccan mosques and *medersas*.

City walls of Safi

During Queen Elizabeth's reign English relations with Morocco were close and cordial. The Queen wanted Moroccan sugar and saltpetre for gunpowder while the Moroccan king wanted British arms and timber for shipbuilding. But, above all, they shared a common enemy, Spain. Envoys went back and forth between London and Marrakesh and were kindly received on both sides; proposals for alliances against Spain and joint expeditions were discussed and agreed; messages were couched in the warmest of terms; yet little joint action was ever actually undertaken. This friendship by epistle died with the two monarchs in 1603 and a quite different chapter in Anglo-Moroccan relations was about to begin.

Piracy was no new game to Queen Elizabeth. She dabbled in it herself and did not discourage her subjects from showing their patriotic zeal in pursuit of the occasional Spanish galleon. Indeed, at the beginning of the seventeenth century, a band of some 2000 English pirates was established in the Moroccan port of Mamora, a little to the north of Salé. During Elizabeth's reign, however, piracy did not ruffle the waters of friendly Anglo-Moroccan relations.

Shortly after her death, however, the Spanish expelled all the remaining Moors from Spain and these exiles settled in Morocco where many of them made their home in Salé and Rabat. They were fired with a hatred of Christians, a desire for revenge and the urgent need to earn a living. They took to piracy like ducks to water and for this their base on the banks of the Bou Regreg river was ideally suited. Soon they were to become the most feared pirates of them all, the notorious Sallee Rovers.

'We were obliged to yield, and were carry'd all prisoners into Sallee, a port belonging to the Moors . . . . I was kept by the captain of the rover as his proper prize . . . .' So began the fabulous adventures of *Robinson Crusoe* by Daniel Defoe. Fact was stranger than fiction in the case of the Sallee Rovers, as many letters and writings from English captives show. The Rov-

ers ransomed their prisoners, if they could, or else sold them into slavery. One, Robert Adams, wrote to his parents begging a ransom and describing his life in New Salé (Rabat) thus: 'My patroone made mee worke at a mill like a horse, from morninge untill night, with chaines uppon my legges, of 36 pounds waights a peece, my meat nothinge but a llitell coarse bread and water, my lodging in a dungeon under ground . . . .'

Of course the Rovers themselves, who were taken prisoner by christian states, did not get away scotfree either. They were made to row the galleys and such numbers were taken that, when an exchange was proposed between French prisoners in Morocco and Moorish prisoners in France, the French saw that they would lose in the deal because they held the greater number of prisoners and did not want their galleys depleted.

Salé was frequently beyond the control of the central government. In the early seventeenth century the Sultan destroyed the pirates there with the help of English shipping. A few years later an English envoy, John Harrison, was negotiating with the pirates for the release of captives, offering British arms in exchange, when the Sultan demanded that he be brought to Court. The pirates refused and declared Salé an independent state which it remained for some fifteen years. During this time many of their most daring raids were undertaken: between 1620 and 1630 they captured over a thousand ships of all nationalities; they raided a village on the coast of Ireland and carried off the population; they raided Plymouth and took 200 captives.

Life changed for the pirates, however, with the accession to power in 1672 of the Sultan Moulay Ismail. A young man of some twenty-six years of age when he came to power, he was to prove stronger and to live longer than any other sultan. Under his rule there was no question of little independent pirate states: soon it was accepted that all captives taken belonged to

Moulay Ismail's *kasbah* of Boulouane

him; soon after, 70 per cent of all cargoes taken belonged to him too.

In 1715 an English boy of eleven, Thomas Pellow, went to sea with his uncle to escape his Latin schooling which he found tedious. They were seized by pirates and sent inland to Meknes, capital city of Moulay Ismail. The Sultan was angry with the pirates' admiral, who had run from a British man-of-war, and ordered him to be immediately beheaded. It was an object lesson for the pirates and Pellow.

Pellow was given to one of the Sultan's sons who forced him to become a Muslim. He became a favourite of the Sultan's and, by dint of courage and intelligence, managed to survive his strange childhood: 'I was oblig'd to walk like one walking on the brink of a dangerous precipice,' he wrote in his memoirs. But better years were ahead: the Sultan appointed him captain of a troop of his guard, gave him a wife and sent him out to command one of the forts which he had built across his land. There the renegade christian troops hunted game in the woods,

enjoyed meals of wild boar and red wine, which the Sultan broadmindedly allowed them, and every now and then went out to suppress rebellions on his behalf. Pellow, however, always dreamed of escape and, after the death of the Sultan, made several abortive attempts to get away through the Portuguese-held port of Mazagan (Al Jadida), through Salé, until finally, in 1736, he made his way to Gibraltar.

Moulay Ismail, the Sultan whom Pellow had served, was the most flamboyant of any Moroccan monarch. He was, indeed, a contemporary of Louis XIV of France, 'le Roi Soleil', and saw himself in a similar role, asking even for the French king's illegitimate daughter to join his numerous harem.

Moulay Ismail was the second sultan of the Alawi dynasty, founded by an Arab tribe of *shurfa* from the desert in the south, from the region of Tafilalet. His older half-brothers established their power throughout the land; he, himself, was dark-skinned, of a slave mother, but he shared his brothers' amazing energy and politi-

37

cal skill, backed by a strong religious faith.

When he came to power he was faced with rebellions which he firmly suppressed; he spent the first quarter century of his reign campaigning throughout the land to establish a peace and security such as the country had probably never known. Thomas Pellow wrote: 'At the Beginning of his Reign, the Roads were so infested with Robbers, that it was dangerous to stir out of the Towns, without being well guarded, but he so well cleared them, that now it is nowhere safer travelling.'

He disliked the city of Fes, which had defied him, and made Meknes his capital. There he spent his long reign of fifty-five years building monumental palaces and city walls of which only 1000 acres of ruins survive. The great city gate, Bab al Mansur, is today the only really fine example of his architecture still intact. These building works were a way of controlling his people by keeping them occupied and impoverished, for it was the people who paid for the buildings.

He was feared by all for his arbitrary cruelty and tyranny. As Pellow remarked: 'He tamed the natural Savageness of his Subjects by showing himself still more savage than they.' Torture and sudden death were everyday occurrences in his palace where his subjects went in fear and trembling, especially if they saw him dressed in yellow, his 'killing colour'. His court executioner, Pellow tells us, was a renegade Englishman, formerly a butcher from Exeter. His court was also described by John Windus who went to Meknes in 1721 to negotiate the release of some 300 British captives. He ruled through his black guard and bred boys for his slave army, arranging mass marriages between his white and black subjects to produce the dark-skinned offspring whom he most favoured: 'Thus he took care to lay the Foundation of his tawny Nurseries . . . (the boys) were so ready to murder and destroy, even while young, that the Alcaydes trembled at the very sight of them.' But the Sultan ruled these wild young creatures with a rod of iron: 'He beat them in the cruellest manner imaginable to try if they were hard.' After his death the security of his realm dissolved in civil strife between his older sons.

Moulay Ismail not only campaigned against his own rebellious subjects; he also harried the foreigners who still held ports around his shores. As chance would have it the British were now numbered among these for they had inherited Tangier.

Tangier had been captured by the Portuguese in 1471 and had been held by them, or by the Spanish, for nearly 200 years. In 1661 Charles I was betrothed to the Portuguese princess, Catherine of Braganza, and Tangier was part of her dowry. Charles was delighted with this strategic gift which he hoped would be a spearhead for British trade and territorial acquisitions in North Africa. But he did not understand the situation. The Portuguese were handing it over with some relief since they were constantly blockaded there by the Spanish from the sea and attacked by the Moroccans on land. The British had to send troops hastily to Tangier to enable the Portuguese to hold it long enough to hand it over. It was a foretaste of things to come. For twenty years the British held Tangier, almost always under siege, at great expense and loss of life. Samuel Pepys was employed for fifteen years as treasurer to deal with the affairs of Tangier. He sailed out to Tangier in 1683 on a secret mission to help arrange the abandonment of the town and destruction of its defences. He was shocked by the strategic weakness of the place: 'But Lord! How could anybody think this place fit to be kept at this charge, that by its being overlooked by so many hills can never be secured against an enemy,' and by the debauchery encouraged by its British governor, Colonel Kirke (later notorious at the battle of Sedgemoor and in the pacification of Somerset). 'On God's account as well as the King's, I think it high time it [Tangier] were dissolved,' remarked Pepys reprovingly. The following year the British left

Walls of Asila

Harbour wall, Tangier

Tangier, watched by Moulay Ismail's troops who ringed the town but did not interfere with the evacuation.

The British experience in Tangier taught the more observant of them something of the character of the Moroccans, a people with whom, over the years, they would have increasing commercial dealings. One of the British commanders, Colonel Sackville, reported home in an attempt to correct the low opinion which his predecessors had expressed of the Moroccans: 'To speake of them as Enimies, I never saw men bolder in the field when they finde it reasonable to fight, nor more prudent to avoid it, when it was wisdom to decline it; nor is there I believe in ye whole race of mankind a more vigilant, hardy, patient and laborious people . . . in their treaty they discourse and debate matters calmly and judiciously, and therefore I see not where the reason of this contempt of them lyes. . . .'

The loss of Tangier was, in a way, only the beginning of British interest in the town. Britain took Gibraltar in 1704 and Tangier became the port from which the garrison at Gibraltar was to receive regular supplies. British merchants settled in the town and a flourishing British community developed there. The British merchants who made their homes in Tangier and Mogador (now Essaouira), Mazagan (now Al Jadida) and Casablanca, found themselves in competition with their traditional rivals, the Spanish and the French. Trade concessions and monopolies were the prizes to be won as well as guaranteed Moroccan supplies for British ships and the garrison in Gibraltar. The British consuls frequently made the long and tiring journey inland on horseback to visit the Sultan at his court in Fes or Marrakesh.

Outstanding among them in the nineteenth

40

century, when the European powers were beginning to take a serious interest in the Moroccan market, were the Drummond Hays. Edward Drummond Hay went to Tangier as Consul-General in 1829. He found the British were more in favour than the other European powers and his long period at the Consulate improved this further but, in 1844, he fell ill. His son, John, a fluent Arabic speaker, asked to be sent to Tangier to help his father. When his father died shortly afterwards he was appointed Consul-General at the age of twenty-nine and stayed there until he was seventy, becoming Minister Resident. Over the years his knowledge of the country deepened and his influence at the court increased to an extent which had never previously been matched by a foreigner. He did not hesitate to speak his mind to the Sultan, nor to advise him for the good of the country. The Sultan would ask for his counsel and thank him for speaking 'like a true friend' when he lectured on the need to improve the administration and check the corruption of the unpaid officials. The anarchy and confusion in Morocco could lead to the loss of her independence, he warned.

The problems which concerned Drummond Hay, and which he had discussed at such length with the Sultans in power during his lifetime, did not diminish after he left Tangier. Indeed, they were aggravated by the accession of a gentle young boy of twelve, Moulay Abdul Aziz, in 1894, and by the lawlessnes into which the country gradually slid. But this was no new state of affairs for Morocco. The country was always difficult to govern; each Sultan over the centuries knew that a rival was waiting in the wings, that in the high mountains and the inaccessible desert beyond were warlike tribes, one of whom at any moment might seize the opportunity to strike northwards and take the rich cities of the plains. The great walls which surround the old towns of Morocco were strictly functional and repeatedly repaired.

The average life-span of a Moroccan dynasty was not very long. Few exerted effective control over the country for much more than a century although some managed to hang on for two centuries. The Alawi family of the present monarch, King Hassan I, has been in power for longer than any other, for three centuries. The Sultan always had to spend much of his time campaigning throughout his realm in order to maintain control. These campaigns were known as *harka,* or burning, for, where the great imperial army moved, the countryside lay stripped bare and dissident towns and villages were laid waste. Life was cheap and rebels were carried off prisoner or executed without more ado. One gruesome side product of the *harka* was the collection of severed rebel heads which adorned the gates and walls of the cities when the army returned. Even at the turn of this century travellers still entered the cities below lines of heads hanging over the gates. Dr Weisgerber of Casablanca found forty heads above the gate of Bab al Had at Rabat in 1897; in 1903 a similar collection taken in the Tafilalet were hanging above the Bab Mahrouq in Fes.

Walter Harris, *The Times* correspondent in Tangier at the turn of the century, travelled throughout the country and knew at first-hand the wildness of tribal life. 'Every tribe had its enemies, every family had its blood feuds and every man his would-be murderer,' he wrote. His own life had hung in the balance when he was taken prisoner by the great brigand chief Raisuli who dominated the northern Rif mountains early this century. He was imprisoned in a room with a headless body but gradually talked his captors round and was finally released by some tribesmen who were his friends. When Raisuli captured two Americans the American fleet steamed into Tangier to demand their release. In return for their freedom the Sultan was obliged to make the brigand governor of the northern region. When he captured the British army officer Caid Maclean he received £20,000 and British nationality in return for his release.

Raisuli was a belated example of the anarchy which, throughout history, had divided the country into *Bled al Makhzen* (the land of government) and *Bled as Siba* (the land of dissidence). Secure in his mountain fastness Raisuli ruled his section of *Bled as Siba*. Harris described how, years later, he watched, concealed from both sides, a Spanish attack on Raisuli's strong-

hold. The Spanish were repelled and, in the evening, alone on the mountain, Harris watched through his binoculars another solitary man surveying, also through binoculars, the distant Spanish troops regrouping for the next day's attack. The man was Raisuli. When the Spanish attacked the following day there was not a soul but themselves on the mountain. Raisuli's band

Those outside were ready to move

Walls defended the city dwellers

had withdrawn to inaccessible heights. And so it had always been. Except in the reign of particularly strong and energetic sultans the mountain and desert tribes could always withdraw to distant fastnesses; their territory remained the land of dissidence.

J. D. H. & J. B. delt.

Tower of the Koutoubia

44

The tribal wars, government *harkas* and tax gathering discouraged the country people of the fertile plains from cultivating their lands. Why work all year to produce a crop which so easily might be taken away in the moment of ripeness? Dr Weisgerber, living in Casablanca in 1900, noted that little of the land round about was cultivated; the country people found it safer to keep flocks and herds and to live in tents themselves. When trouble came they could always move on. The cultivator cannot leave; he is tied to his crop.

Human factors were far from being the only ones to discourage agriculture. A good crop was just as likely to fall victim to a swarm of locusts as to a hostile tribe. Until very recently locusts were the bane of the Moroccan peasant, covering the ground in a thick layer and stripping every growing thing from plants and trees.

While locusts could cause famine in the land, a far more deadly cause of famine was the complete failure of the crop due to drought. When droughts continued for several years in succession the country people died of hunger. In a weak state they drifted into the towns hoping for help, but there fell victims to disease; thus famines were nearly always followed by plagues. A particularly terrible famine struck the country between 1776-82; it was followed by another famine and a plague which raged from 1797 to 1800. Nearly half the population of the country died; the towns were left empty and in the countryside the few survivors tried to keep life going and became rich on the inheritance left by their dead neighbours.

An Englishman, James Jackson, lived through that plague in Mogador. He described how the people were suddenly struck with shivering or delirium and then became covered in carbuncles, spots and boils. Most died within a day or so; very few survived. He decided that only very close contact could transmit the plague and allowed no one to approach nearer than a yard or so. He survived, unscathed, although his cook died.

Even until quite recently the familiar pattern of drought followed by plague could still repeat itself. Patrick Turnbull tells of the lack of rain in the Marrakesh region in the winters of 1935 and 1936. Starving country people dragged themselves into the town from the mountains and the plain. Pathetic columns of dying men, women and children trekked along the roads and tracks; skeletal figures begged for a crust of bread in the city streets. The soup kitchens and charity collections could not touch the extent of the problem. In the winter of 1937 an epidemic of typhus (which is carried by lice) broke out in the city. Turnbull went into the city centre and was shocked when a beggar fell dead at his feet; in a deserted courtyard he saw the body of a man and a small girl dying all alone. Appalled he drove away from the doomed city, the unending funeral chant ringing in his ears.

Mausoleum of King Muhammad V founder of the modern state

46

3 Modern Morocco

At the beginning of this century Morocco was ruled by the young Sultan Abd al Aziz who had come to the throne as a boy. He had no taste for the job – 'You don't know how weary I am of being Sultan,' he once confessed to Walter Harris – and he was always surrounded by scheming courtiers. His real love was for the new inventions of Europe and he spent far more than his country could afford on carriages, for which there were no roads, cameras, telephones, telescopes, bicycles and boats, all laboriously transported overland to be used for a while then abandoned. The Europeans at his court vied with each other in encouraging these extravagances.

As Morocco's finances foundered the predatory Europeans moved closer to establishing control. Rivals for a share in Morocco were the French, who already ruled Algeria, the Spanish, who had held for centuries Ceuta, Melilla and the islands of Al Hoceima in the north, the British and the Germans. Eventually, Britain ceded her interest in Morocco in exchange for France's dropping her interest in Egypt; the French swapped with the Germans their rights in the Congo for the Germans' interests in Morocco, while the Spanish claim to an interest in the north was supported by the other European states to prevent the French taking all.

The excuse to move into Morocco came in 1907 when nine Europeans working on the construction of a port in Casablanca were murdered. The neighbouring tribes seized the opportunity of the ensuing disturbances to attack the town, but the French were as quick as they were. French ships bombarded the town to keep the tribes at bay and French troops landed. Casablanca and the surrounding countryside were soon in French hands. When, four years later, the tribes besieged Fes the Sultan asked for French help and in 1912 the French Protectorate was signed. Spain was given control of the north, as far south as the Oued Loukkos where the old frontier posts can still be seen on the main roads, and Tangier became an international city.

In Europe it was the eve of the First World War and in Morocco the tribes were as turbulent and as rebellious as ever – more so, perhaps, for the centuries of struggle against the Spanish and Portuguese had left them strongly anti-Christian; they resisted the French with all their strength. But in the twentieth century the cards were no longer evenly stacked: European military training and equipment far outclassed anything which the Berber tribes had known. Nevertheless, the position might have been disastrous for France had she not then sent out the greatest of her governors, General (later Marshal), Lyautey.

Lyautey's first problem was to gain control of the country. He was always short of troops, particularly during the First World War, and was usually short of money also. At one time he wrote home in despair that he understood that he could not have men but, if he were refused money too, he wondered by what magic they thought he might pacify the country. In fact, he followed in the footsteps of the great sultans of the past, displaying immense energy, always on the move himself (on his signet ring was carved a line from Shelley: 'The soul's joy lies in doing') and displaying strength in order not to have to use it.

Each step was studied and prepared scrupulously in advance; tribes were subdued with as little armed force as possible and were immediately offered material benefits in the hope of winning their allegiance. Nevertheless, it was not until 1934 that the mountains were completely pacified; twenty years later the nationalist revolt against the French, which was to sweep the country to independence, was already brewing.

Lyautey effectively ruled Morocco until 1926 when he returned, 'a prophet without honour', to France. He had throughout upheld the value of Moroccan culture and institutions. He had decreed that the old Moroccan cities be left untouched and that new French towns be built only outside their walls; he had insisted that non-Muslims be refused entry to mosques; he tried to create a Franco-Moroccan educational system for the children of the elite; and he always respected the prestige of the Sultan of whom he said, 'I am honoured to count myself the first of His Majesty's servants.'

During the First World War Lyautey was obliged to accept a solution, for control of the High Atlas and the southern part of the country, which had in it the seeds of future strife and contributed to the final downfall of the French. The mountains were dominated at the time by three powerful warlords of whom the greatest was Madani el Glaoui. Operating from his fortress *kasbah* of Telouet (near the present Tizi n'Tishka pass) he controlled much of the Atlas and the city of Marrakesh. France was able to hold the south with minimum expense and loss of life, thanks to the help of these warlords and especially of Madani and his brother Thami. Madani died in 1918; his brother lived on as Pasha of Marrakesh and was a firm supporter of the French until 1955 when the French decided he was no longer an asset to them. He died soon after in disgrace and a new verb *'glaouiser'* – 'to be betrayed' – crept into the French language.

The material achievements of the French in Morocco in the brief forty-four years of their rule were extraordinary. They built roads and railways and opened passes across the high mountains to give access to the south; they established peace throughout the realm and disarmed the tribes. Above all they developed agriculture and brought the great plains under cultivation; the cities were enlarged and the beginnings of local industries were established.

Yet, as one scholar remarked, much was done for the Moroccan people but little was done by them. Agricultural development, especially, was in the hands of French colonists who bought or otherwise obtained huge tracts of land on which they worked with untiring zeal. Commerce and industry were also foreign dominated, with Europeans controlling 80 per cent of all enterprises. During the Protectorate Europeans had the lion's share of education: 8200 students graduated from the European population of eventually 300,000 in Morocco, 775 from the Moroccan Jews (who numbered about the same as the Europeans) and only 640 from the eventually 12 million Moroccan Muslims.

Such inequality led educated nationalists to campaign against the French who made the old mistake of imprisoning the moderate nationalists only to find their place taken by more radical and militant protesters. Over the years, also, the nationalists acquired a leader of stature in the person of the young Sultan Muhammad v. Muhammad had been chosen as Sultan in 1927, at the age of seventeen, on the death of his father. He showed a natural political talent and began to seek close links with the Berber tribes of the mountains. The people of Morocco started to rally round him.

In 1953 the French, in alliance with the Glaoui, decided that the only way to stop this wave of popularity was to exile the Sultan; Muhammad v was sent to Madasgascar. The move was a miscalculation: serious disturbances and attacks on the French population broke out

LE BOULEVARD DU 4ᵉ ZOUAVES EN 1889

Photos FLANDRIN

LE BOULEVARD DU 4ᵉ ZOUAVES EN 1938

Reprod. interd.

3.—CASABLANCA AUTREFOIS & AUJOURD'HUI

across the country. At the end of 1955 Muhammad was restored to his throne; Thami al Glaoui, an old and dying man, crawled on his knees to beg forgiveness; and in 1956 Morocco gained independence led by Muhammad v as its much-loved sovereign.

For some time the dream of independence had served to unite Moroccans of all backgrounds, but the independent state would be no more easy to govern than Morocco had ever been and its architect, Muhammad v, was not destined to live long to guide the nation which he had created. He was succeeded in 1961 by his son, King Hassan II, who was faced with the task of creating a modern framework for the new state.

In the past, Morocco had been ruled by an absolute monarch whose power was, as we have seen, more or less absolute according to the strength of his rule. He was always, however, acknowledged as the leader of the faithful and the Alawi family, who are *shurfa,* descendants of the Prophet Muhammad, are believed to possess especial *baraka.* The King leads his people in prayer as well as in government or in battle.

Muhammad v introduced a constitutional monarchy and ruled with the help of ministers, consulting the wishes of the people through representatives of the main political parties and sectors of the population. King Hassan II has attempted to find a balance between King and parliament which would be acceptable to the people and, at the same time, capable of carrying the country forward on the road to development and economic self-sufficiency.

The path was not easy. In the early 1970s instability increased and the monarchy was shaken by two attempted *coups d'état.* These both failed, largely due to the King's own personal courage and coolness. A new constitution in 1972 and the Moroccanization of industry and commerce helped regain the support of the people. This was consolidated in 1975 in dramatic fashion by the *Marche Verte,* the unarmed invasion of the Spanish Sahara to the south by ordinary Moroccan people from all walks of life.

Sculpted cedar-wood in an old college

The success of this venture gained for Morocco control of large tracts of desert territory; for the King it won the genuine support and affection of his people.

Today, authority is in the hands of the King and parliament, a body freely elected from candidates of the numerous political parties. The King appoints a government of ministers to carry out his instructions and to draft the country's laws and development plans which it must submit to parliament for approval.

The overriding problems facing the government are the urgent need to produce sufficient jobs and food for the rapidly increasing population of the country and to provide education for a people who, until very recently, had next to none. In past centuries Moroccan children,

50

mostly the boys, were given a traditional religious education in the Koran schools where they learnt to read and write, do some arithmetic and, above all, to recite the Koran by heart. When a boy could recite the complete Koran he was escorted home on horseback and his father gave a party for his schoolfellows. The French introduced some modern education but it was available only to the fortunate few. By 1940 3 per cent of Moroccan children were in school; by 1953 the nationalists estimated that 6 per cent were at school. Illiteracy was, and still is, widespread, but today many of the children are learning to read.

After independence immense efforts were made to provide schooling throughout the country, in small village schools in the mountains and the plain as well as in the huge urban schools. Rather over half the children of primary age are now in school but the problem of providing teachers and teaching materials, and of establishing a language in which to teach, has been great. During the Protectorate schooling was in French and educated Moroccans are bilingual. Moroccan teachers had themselves been educated in French and text books were only available in French. Today, the first years of primary schooling are in Arabic but, once the child has mastered the difficult skill of reading Arabic, he must set about French, for science subjects, among others, are still taught in French in secondary schools and universities. Many French teachers are still employed in these institutions.

Schooling for girls, although not as widespread as that for boys, has been eagerly accepted. The first school for girls in the countryside was opened in 1933. A few years later the nationalists were demanding schools for girls in their campaign against the French, while parents were ready to approve an education which, it seemed, could increase the dowry their daughter could command on marriage. Most Moroccan schools are co-educational and today a third of their pupils are girls.

Crowding into the Towns

Every year there are more mouths to feed in Morocco and every year more of her people make their way into the towns. Although the area of cultivated land is being continually extended it cannot support the increasing numbers of people in the villages; those who find themselves without land or work hope for a better living in the cities. They are joined by others seeking educational opportunities for their children or medical care.

Moroccan towns have grown like giant mushrooms in recent years and their growth is very visible. At the beginning of the century the towns still huddled within their walls and the city gates clanged shut at night; few citizens chose to live outside the walls. But the narrow streets and close-packed houses inside the walls were inadequate to cope with the growing population, although they are far more densely inhabited now than they ever were. Many of the old *medinas* are now harbouring four times as many inhabitants as they were built to do.

Casablanca has seen the most frightening increase of population and, although other towns have not mushroomed to quite the same extent, it is, nevertheless, an example of what is happening, on a smaller scale, all over Morocco. At the beginning of the nineteenth century James Jackson put the population of Casablanca, then 'in ruins and consisting of only several huts', at 1,000. Leo Africanus, three centuries before, had described Anfa (as it was then called)

as totally ruined by the Portuguese to such an extent that he saw no hope that it would ever be inhabited again. But he was no prophet. By the mid-nineteenth century 4000 people had made their homes there; by 1900 there were 20,000. Today, nearly 3 million people are living in the city which has become the country's commercial and industrial capital and largest town by far.

Happily, throughout the land, the old towns have been preserved within their walls and new districts have been built alongside them. Even in Casablanca, where development has been most abrupt, the old *medina* remains, a little huddle of winding lanes beside the port, the old city wall running around two sides of it at least. Elsewhere, the red or gold, mud-built city walls are generally intact, pierced here and there by the need to take a broad street capable of containing today's heavy traffic.

Traffic has become as much of a problem in Morocco as it has in Europe. City streets are crowded and the rule of priority from the right is a continual hazard. Many Moroccans ride mopeds (which are notably less well-disciplined than their donkeys) and accidents are frequent. While the long straight country roads are often refreshingly little used, traffic is dense on the north-south route of Tangier–Rabat–Casablanca–Marrakesh. These roads are especially dangerous at sundown when the country people return to their villages with unlighted carts and tractors, donkeys and flocks of animals.

The streets in the modern parts of the cities are wide and pleasantly laid out. They are often lined with trees, stately palms or shady eucalyptus, pink-berried pepper trees, or the beautiful blue-flowered jacaranda which transforms the streets of Marrakesh in the month of May. In summer, the city streets are alive with birds for swallows, swifts and house-martins arrive in spring in incredible numbers and swirl and swoop over the thoroughfares so that, at times, the sky is almost black with them and the air vibrant with their shrill cries. Above them,

throughout the early half of the year, glide the majestic storks who come to Morocco at Christmas-time to nest on old buildings and rear their leggy fledglings before taking off again in July. They are welcomed and protected by the people who regard a stork's nest on their buildings as a lucky omen.

Near the centres of the towns the streets are packed with people, drifting along in the warm sunshine or, in summer, enjoying the shade of the covered alleys of the old *souqs*. Groups of schoolchildren in pink or blue or white pinafores bring a splash of uniform colour to the motley throng. Here and there a woman or child moves carefully, a tray covered with a clean cloth balanced on their head, on the way to the baker's oven with the family supply of bread or pastries to be cooked. Along the pavement edge a man pushes an old bicycle, calling *'biyes, biyes'* – the old clothes man, asking for people's cast-offs.

The crowds, who have come so recently to the city, have difficulty finding a home. They move in with relatives already there, sharing perhaps ten or more to a room. Or they build themselves a little shack in the shanty towns which have grown up beside all the big cities. Life there retains something of the personal quality of the village but the poverty and lack of services make it a struggle. The lucky ones may find a home in some of the extensive new government housing developments; whole suburbs of low-cost apartment blocks have been built to rent or to be bought on very favourable terms but, as these absorb newcomers from the countryside, they are replaced by others and so the problem continues.

The difficulty of finding work is no less than that of finding a home. Newcomers from the country rarely have the skills needed to command a job in the city and many of them remain unemployed, depending on a relative to keep them and their children. People who do have work can easily find themselves keeping half-a-dozen relatives as well as their own family. Divorced mothers, far from their own families,

find it particularly hard to support their children. Small wonder that those who despair of working may try to earn a pittance begging, especially as Muslims are constrained to give alms to the poor as a basic religious duty. Some of the less scrupulous become adept at picking pockets; in a crowd the wise keep a firm hand on their wallet.

Leisure is precious and the climate makes spare time as agreeable for the Moroccans as it is for visiting holiday-makers. Pavement cafés are filled with men sipping cups of black coffee or glasses of sweet mint tea. Patches of wasteland are as popular as well-equipped football pitches with youths and boys, for whom football is not only a universal sport but also a way of life. They spend their evenings and weekends training along the suburban roadways or on the sandy beaches. James Jackson, 200 years ago, remarked that football was by far the favourite game; its popularity has been on the increase ever since.

A favourite outing for city dwellers, young or old, male or female, is to the *hammam* or Turkish bath. Moroccan towns have, for many centuries, been well supplied with these steam baths (Leo Africanus counted 100 in Fes in 1500); to these the citizens go once a week and while away happy hours, conversing with neighbours and friends as they cook gently in the hot humid atmosphere. Separate baths serve men and women and the bathers strip naked, or virtually so, on entering. They move from one tiled room to another, each hotter than the last and, in the hot rooms, are scrubbed with soap and a rough flannel by the bath attendants. It seems, at first, incongruous, to watch women, who are covered from head to toe with faces carefully veiled in the streets, sitting around stark naked in the *hammam* and chatting with complete unconcern. They leave with a feeling of cleanliness such as nothing else can produce, not a scrap of grime having escaped the prolonged steaming and rough scrubbing.

Shopping, like bathing, is a veritable experi-

54

ence in Morocco. One faces not only the excitement of an exotic whirl through a range of languages – Arabic, French, Berber, English, German or whatever the shopkeeper deems appropriate from his stock in trade – but also the challenge of deciphering the currency. The Moroccan coin is the dirham (in 1980 worth about 12p), but few Moroccan shopkeepers seem to have accepted this. If you ask the price of an article in English you might get the answer in dirhams though the shopkeeper will probably double his price); if you ask in French (thus implying a foreigner who at least knows the country and so commands a lower price), the answer will come back in old French francs, a hundred to the dirham; if you ask in Arabic (which here is *ish hal?*), thus commanding the lowest price of all, the answer will come in riyals, of which there are twenty to the dirham.

Rapid calculation is required to sort out the currency in which the price has been given, for it is never specifically stated, and to calculate a good offering price – perhaps half or a third the asking price. A lengthy period of haggling will end in an agreed price somewhere between that of buyer and seller. Unfortunately, no ready reckoner of how much to reduce the asked price can be given. A shopkeeper, who thinks he spots a greenhorn, may ask ten times the real price; another may not be interested in bargaining at all and may ask his final price, or nearly so, from the outset. The only sure way to proceed is to visit a government *cooperative artisanal,* where goods are sold at fixed prices, as a start. Then you should enquire the asking price for the same object in numerous stalls, being willing to move on to the next stall if the first does not lower his price. A morning spent thus will certainly procure the very best price for the leather belt or striped blanket or brown cape which you covet. With less time at your disposal you will have to accept something a little above absolute bargain prices.

Of course, in the cities, there are also modern shops, supermarkets and department stores, where goods are bought at fixed prices and there is little scope for bargaining. They are part of the modern life in the main streets of the city centres or in the residential suburbs. In these new districts villas in super-modern styles are springing up alongside more conventional ones built in the 1920s and 1930s or later. In such areas a house built thirty years ago is regarded as old.

In either case these suburban villas have broken away from the traditional styles of Moroccan town houses of which beautiful examples still exist in many of the old towns. Such houses are hard, if not impossible, to spot from the outside, for all town houses, rich and poor, presented a more or less blank and poor-looking wall to the street. A glimpse of the interior through the doorway is also not to be expected: the entrance to an old house always takes an immediate right-angled turn just inside the door and then another, which brings one into the central courtyard, completely protected from the curious gaze of passers-by.

Moroccan houses are all centred on their little courtyard. As Elizabeth Murray, who lived in Tangier in the 1840s noticed, they were designed very like the Roman houses of Pompeii. Had she visited Morocco today she could have seen the same Roman design in the impressive ruins of Volubilis, near Meknes; there, one can walk into house after house and admire the central courtyard, the columns which once supported its portico, and the exquisite mosaics which tiled the floors.

In the simple houses of the Moroccan *medinas* the walls are painted white, the rooms are long and narrow, for rafters to span wide rooms were few and far between, and the lower part of the walls and often the floors are covered with faience tiles. The roofs are flat and the women spend much of their day on the roof-tops. The windows usually have wrought-iron grilles and wooden shutters, but glass was a rare luxury.

Wealthy town houses, while built to the same basic plan and appearing no different from those of the poor from the outside, were richly decor-

A 1930's villa

ated within. Here, in courtyards and rooms, the lower part of the walls was covered with multi-coloured mosaic glazed tiles known as *zellijs* and, above them, with sculpted plaster stucco work; the ceilings were of cedar wood painted in deep greens, reds and golds. Doors were high, swinging on a pivot and painted in geometric or arabesque designs.

In the courtyards a marble fountain splashed a refreshing stream into a marble basin at its foot. A fig tree and grape vine might provide shade while, in bigger courtyards, there might be

around the wall. Goods were stored in painted wooden chests and objects displayed on sets of painted wooden shelves. The effect of the painted woodwork of ceilings and furnishings was bright and colourful, while the tiles and fountains created a cool and restful atmosphere.

Modern villas have abandoned the tradition of a house which turns in on itself and where life is lived in a central courtyard. They, on the contrary, are set in their own garden, with large windows looking out onto the lawn and, where they have balconies, these too are on the outside of the building, looking over the garden. Furnishings and layout of these houses follow standard European lines, but many Moroccans cling to tradition in the design of one room, the 'Moroccan Room', which serves as sitting or dining room. Here, the walls are tiled with *zellijs* and sculpted stucco work and furnishing is a bench along the wall with a flat mattress and large cushions against which guests may lean.

The gardens outside are a mass of flowers for most of the year. Practically all flowers, it seems, grow and flourish in Morocco. Daffodils, tulips, violets, jasmine, irises and roses evoke northern Europe; while hibiscus, papyrus, bougainvillaea, canna, heavy-scented datura and the bright yellow puff-balls of mimosa, recall the Mediterranean or more tropical climates. Geraniums in every shade of white, pink and red are the town garden flowers par excellence. They flourish in window-boxes and courtyards, they climb high up walls and trees and there is never a week when one cannot find at least a few plants in flower; in spring, the suburban streets are ablaze with them. Trees and shrubs grow rapidly, lawns remain green throughout the summer if watered, plants flower early and long – all in all, Morocco is a gardener's paradise, the one place where those whose fingers were never in the least green may believe themselves true experts.

In the modern districts of the main towns new hotels have been built to international standards and more are under construction. Hotels in the

orange or grapefruit trees. A balcony often ran around the court at first-floor level and in some town houses there might be another floor, also with a balcony, above that.

The rooms were simply furnished, seating consisting of cushions or covered benches

Fountain in the courtyard of Dar Batha, Fes

four- and five-star categories offer the businessman and tourist very acceptable standards of comfort while smaller hotels and inns, with a lower or no star rating, are widely available for the more adventurous, at extremely reasonable rates. Hotel room prices are govern-

ment controlled and are modest compared with rates in many countries.

Morocco has a long tradition in the hotel business. Leo Africanus recorded that there were some 200 inns in Fes in the early sixteenth century, well built and equipped with drains and

58

We can deduce from Leo Africanus's more detailed account what 'simple' might indicate: the inns had no furniture, but the traveller was given a straw mat and, if he brought in his own food, it would be cooked for him.

Moroccan hoteliers have come a long way since then and some of the country's more famous hotels offer refined accommodation in an exquisite setting (though, alas, no longer for 2 pence a night). The hotels which have made the greatest reputation are among the older ones and all have particularly fine surroundings: best known is the Mamounia in Marrakesh. This hotel is situated in a beautiful garden, just inside the old city walls. It was Winston Churchill's favourite holiday place during and after the Second World War.

Taroudant, an ancient walled town in the far south, has two beautiful and original hotels where connoisseurs of comfort can enjoy the delights of permanent summer weather throughout the winter. One, the Palais Salaam, is an old palace built up against the ramparts and around a series of enchanting little courtyards, heavy with the scent of flowering trees and shrubs. The other, the Gazelle d'Or, consists of a chain of exquisite little pavilions set in an attractive park. Its food, for which it was once justly famed, is now rather ordinary, but it still offers an idyllically peaceful setting for a holiday in the sun. Closer to the beaten track and more modern than any of these other hotels, the well-run Miramar in Mohammedia near Casablanca stands beside the sea in delightful gardens and close to one of the country's best golf courses.

For those who like their holiday to be a gastronomic experience some of the best meals may still be found in remote little country inns whose owners make the most of the game and other produce available locally. A recent *Guide Bleu*'s star ratings for restaurants can lead to some unexpected delights.

running water, to a standard which he had hardly ever seen in Italy. Lancelot Addison, in the 1660s, remarked that *funduqs* (inns) had recently become widely available and that the costs were very reasonable – 2 pence each for a man and his horse for a simple night's lodging.

The Koutoubia, Marrakesh

4 Antique Cities of the Plain

From ancient times until the present century Morocco's greatest cities were sited well in the interior of the country, safe from foreign assault by sea. Their high golden walls rose from the plain which they dominated. Their merchant citizens were the prosperous sector of the country's population, quick to close their city gates and to defend their interests against the numerous attacks to which they were subjected over the centuries.

These cities, Fes, Marrakesh and Meknes, were the sultans' capitals for over a thousand years. Sometimes one city was supreme, sometimes another; at times, even, rival sultans would be installed in competing capitals, glowering across at each other and seeking to launch the assault which would prove final.

Today, the city walls are crumbling gently, their purpose lost in the modern world. Swifts make their nests in the holes, which appear in regular lines, marking the places where the wooden mould was set in their construction long ago. Near the tourist gateways they are carefully patched and maintained; there is thus hope that they will survive and not be replaced simply by a ring road as have been the city walls of northern Europe.

Above the old walls the flat roofs of the high, close-built, town houses can be glimpsed: in the northern towns of Fes and Meknes they are white, grey or beige; in the south, at Marrakesh, they have the deep terracotta colouring of the local landscape and the Atlas mountains. Outside the walls lie the garden suburbs of the new towns with their wide tree-lined boulevards, green parks and flower-filled private gardens.

Although the residents may now prefer to live in the new suburbs if they have the means it is the ancient cities inside the walls which draw visitors from all over the world. These old cities consist of a maze of little lanes and it is often useful to take a guide to show you around this veritable rabbit-warren and to point out the interesting monuments. You will be assailed by a horde of boys insisting on being your guide as soon as you approach any of the well-known old towns. The best solution is to take an official guide, who can be hired through the hotel or tourist office, for a half day at a time. For shorter trips choose a boy small enough to control in case your visit ends in dispute, and agree a price before you set out. If you do not want a guide you can always ask the way of shopkeepers. Do not be put off by the strangeness, or the insistence of the would-be guides; the old towns are well worth visiting. It is they, without a doubt, which are Morocco's five-star attraction and greatest of them all is Fes. Set in a landscape of rolling, olive-clad hills, hot in summer and cold in winter, Fes stands today a living relic of a long-lost world.

Fes, a Step Back into the Past

A film of the *Arabian Nights* was recently shot in the lanes and alleys of the old *medina* of Fes. It was an appropriate choice for Fes must be one of the very few cities in the world where so extensive an area has remained unchanged from the Middle Ages. You can walk for hours through the narrow, winding passages which serve as streets, and still have seen but a tiny fraction of the town.

View over old Fes

These lanes range in width from that of a reasonable alleyway, along which perhaps four or five people might walk abreast, to others the width of an average passage in a house. They are not far removed from such in atmosphere either, for the narrower lanes often plunge beneath the buildings in long enclosed tunnels. The only traffic in this maze of lanes consists of donkeys and mules with laden paniers who manage to supply all the needs of the old town. They carry in bricks and other building materials, they carry out the rubbish, they are piled high with the slimy skins destined for the tanneries. Their owners call a warning *'Bālak'* – 'Watch out'. To pass them in the narrower lanes you must often squeeze into a doorway. The walls are rubbed shiny by pedestrians and animals; where the plaster has fallen one glimpses the herring-bone brickwork of ancient walls.

Underfoot the lanes are paved with cobbles; they rise and descend, following the contours of the hillsides, and drop steeply to the river bed which cuts across the town. In steeper places the streets are set in a series of wide, shallow steps. Shafts of sunlight glance into the chiaroscuro of the wider lanes which are often roofed over with a lattice-work of bamboo fronds; into the narrower lanes the sun never penetrates. Here and there an open square offers a pool of light, though often filtered through the leaves of a spreading tree. The medieval town builders sought relief from the hot summer sun and protection from the winds which cut through the streets of the new town in winter.

At street corners and in the squares are set ornately tiled drinking fountains; their canopies, supported by carved cedar-wood beams, are covered with curved green tiles. Water was piped from early times throughout the town and drains carried waste water back to the *oued*. Most beautiful of the fountains is that in the little square of the *Najjarin* (the carpenters). Its waters

Najjarin fountain, Fes

splash before an arch of blue-and-green faience tiles under a heavy canopy of carved cedar wood. To one side of the fountain is the heavy, richly ornamented gateway of an eighteenth-century inn, now used as a students' hostel.

In the narrow alleys leading off the square carpenters chip away at sweet-smelling thuya wood; they saw and chisel while their toes turn handles which emerge rapidly under their blades. In a parallel lane metal workers hammer incised silver patterns into huge iron vases, model swans and old-style stirrups. The speed with which they execute their delicate work is astonishing.

These lanes of craftsmen are typical of the old town of Fes. Throughout the town are tiny booths and workshops where men and boys labour at their minute tasks, hammering patterns on metal trays, beating a delicate gilt-inlay pattern into coloured leather purses or folders, weaving woollen *jellabas* and blankets, sewing the corded threadwork onto *kaftans* and gowns. Often their workshops are barely large enough to turn around in, they may be set below street level, the lighting is exiguous. Yet the craftsmen keep at their tasks, their fingers moving rapidly, oblivious to the gaze of curious passers-by.

In some of the alleys down by the river other artisans are producing more colourful products. In a dark and muddy lane near the metal workers' square are the dyers' vats where bulky skeins of wool or silk are dipped into huge metal cauldrons and hauled out brilliant red, blue, yellow or purple. Colours almost as striking as these are stirred further along the *oued* in the stone vats of the tanners. There, dozens of vats are set side by side and the workers, clothed only in brief shorts and vest, trample the skins down into a variety of coloured dyes. On the walls and roofs around the tanneries yellow, red or green skins are hung to dry. Others are laid out, a rainbow of colours, on the green hillside to the north of town and collected up again at nightfall.

The sounds and smells of the old town blend with the sights in this overwhelming impression of an intensive, medieval existence. The hammering and banging of the craftsmen, the urgent call of '*Balak*' from the donkey men and the cries of the street traders, are over-ridden five times a day by the *muezzins* calling the faithful to prayer from the minarets of the town's numerous mosques. The sweet smell of freshly cut wood in the carpenters' stalls blends with the smells of incense and spices and perfumes in the *souq al attarin*. Down in the *oued* the smells are less enticing though no less authentic; here the medieval drainage system makes itself known while the sickly smell of curing skins from the tanneries is one of the most nauseous with which men may have to work.

At night the different sections of the old town can be closed off from each other by heavy wooden gates. From the first, Fes was built in clearly separate sections: the Andalus district and Fes al Bali, each with its own town wall, were the original sections. Later were added Fes al Jadid (New Fes — but built in 1276) and the Kasbah des Cherarda, also with their own walls. Today the city gates are no longer closed at night but the district gates may be; one evening in Ramadan I was hurrying down the main street of the Grand Talaa in Fes al Bali when the street suddenly stopped in front of me. A night watchman with a huge bunch of keys remarked that he had just locked all the gates in that district and that I would have to work my way around it to the outside world.

Old Fes, indeed, has changed little in the past 500 years since it was described in brilliant detail by an amazing personality whom we know as Leo Africanus. He was born Hassan ben Muhammad al Wazzan az Zayyati in Granada, somewhere around 1490. It was not a propitious start for, within a few years, the Catholic kings had taken the city and his family fled to Fes. There he enjoyed a good Islamic education and began to travel with caravans, leaving the city, to Timbuctoo and the east. Soon he was travelling on diplomatic or commercial missions for

The tanneries

Gateway of an old *funduq*

the Sultan. On his return from one mission to the orient, during which he had made the muslim pilgrimage to Mecca, he was captured off Tunisia by Sicilian pirates and, as a prisoner of outstanding learning and culture, was presented to Pope Leo X, John of Medici. Under pressure from the latter he finally accepted (as Thomas Pellow was later to do) a change of religion. He was baptised personally by the Pope who gave him his own christian names.

Leo soon mastered Italian and sat down to write, in detail, an account of the countries he had visited. Perhaps the most interesting section of *The History and Description of Africa,* since it was the part which he knew best, is his description of Fes.

In the town of his day water was conducted to most of the houses and drains carried the waste to the river. There were 150 public conveniences and 100 public baths. The latter were identical to the *hammams* of today with cool, medium and hot rooms, the heating being provided by dung fires. Leo noted that the young people stripped stark naked in the baths and walked around quite unabashed, but that older men modestly fastened a towel around their loins.

The old inns, *funduqs,* which today have become warehouses or carpet shops, provided lodgings for travellers and for widowers of the town who would otherwise have been alone. They were built around a large central courtyard with stabling and stores on the ground floor and rooms for the travellers above. Unfortunately, some of the *funduqs,* Leo remarked, had become houses of ill repute, frequented by men dressed as women and by ladies of easy virtue.

He described the stalls which lined the street then, as they do now: surprising, perhaps, are his comments on the flower shops and his remarks that those who drank wine always liked to have flowers near them, and on the milk shops where 23,000 litres of milk were sold daily. Then, as now, there were stalls selling cooked meats and other foods; he felt it necessary to describe how meats were roasted in

ovens since his European readers knew only spit roasting. He talked of the crafts practised in the town and commented especially on the weavers who had some 520 workshops. There were said to be 20,000 weavers in the town, he noted.

The religious buildings of Fes were as important in Leo's time as they are today. There were, he said, some 700 mosques and oratories and most important of these, of course, was the Qarawiyin. This great mosque, the largest in Africa, is centrally situated in the old town at the hub of the city's life. It was founded in the ninth century (by refugees from Qairawan in Tunisia) and was enlarged and embellished by successive monarchs over the centuries. Its green tiled roof is supported on 270 pillars and it is lighted by huge bronze chandeliers. Non-Muslims may not enter this or other mosques but, from the lanes alongside, one may catch a glimpse of the great courtyard. This is at its most moving during Ramadan when the court is filled with people, sitting, conversing or kneeling in prayer, while the children run about among their elders. In the covered lanes alongside the walls candle sellers offer long, decorated, coloured candles for use in the mosque.

The Qarawiyin, from the earliest times, was the centre of the city's intellectual life and of a university which is, perhaps, the oldest in the world. In the Middle Ages university professors and students were well paid, thanks to generous endowments, and the university attracted intellectuals from all the known world. Even a Pope (Sylvester II who was Pope from 999 to 1003) is believed to have studied there.

Attached to this and other mosques were a series of *medersas,* theological colleges in which students lived and studied. These are still some of the finest buildings to be seen in old Moroccan towns and Fes is particularly rich in them for each new dynasty in the past sought to add their own. The fourteenth-century Attarin *medersa,* near the Qarawiyin mosque, is perhaps the most exquisite of them all. Its small courtyard, with round marble pool and fountain, is tiled in black and white and the lower part of its walls are covered with green, blue, brown and yellow mosaic tiles. Delicately carved stucco with Quranic inscriptions encases the walls above the tiles and below the carved, deep-brown cedar wood which supports the green-tiled roof. Slender marble columns around the courtyard support a portico whose arches are outlined with carved cedar while, at one end of the courtyard, a large arch with stucco stalactites leads into a prayer hall lit by a huge fourteenth-century chandelier.

Although it is the smallest of the *medersas* the Attarin college is typical of the style of them all. In the nearby Cherratin *medersa* the plan of the students' rooms can be studied. Many of these small, cell-like rooms, with their glass-less windows, had been divided in later times by the addition of a wooden floor, making each two-storey; they are grouped on the upper floor around the courtyard and around small light-wells in each corner of the building. Leo Africanus tells a story of the richly decorated fourteenth-century Bou Inania *medersa* that, when the building was complete and the Sultan asked for the accounts, he looked through them amazed, then threw the account book into the canal saying: 'An expensive thing which is beautiful is not expensive; one cannot pay too much for a thing which pleases.' His building has pleased many thousands over the past 600 years.

The great days of the university were over, however, by Leo Africanus's time. He tells how civil wars had reduced the revenues from the estates which financed the colleges, how students were no longer given bursaries and how teachers' pay had diminished. After his time the decline continued and the colleges fell into disrepair. Today they are empty of students but are being extensively repaired as important monuments of the old towns. The university, however, which concentrates on theology, has been revived in this century and now has such faculties as mathematics, medicine and law.

The town of Fes itself had followed the downward fortunes of its university. After the rise of Meknes it was no longer the capital of the land and, although the Sultan chose it as his capital at the end of the last century and the beginning of this, it was soon to be superseded by Rabat. As the centre of activity moved to the sea coast at Rabat, Tangier and, ultimately, Casablanca, the merchant families, who had made the prosperity of Fes, left their homes in the old town.

These families, a mere handful, with names which often begin with Ben (Benkirane, Benjelloun, Benchekroune, etc.,), interrelated by marriage and with close commercial links as well, have established themselves in their new homes as one of the major powers in the land. At the end of the past century, and the beginning of this, many of them settled a branch of their family in Manchester for the cotton trade. It is still common to meet elderly Fasis (people of Fes) who were born in Manchester or whose parents or grandparents lived there. They still have a soft spot for their adopted home which they left when the cotton market collapsed in the 1930s with the introduction of cheap Japanese cotton. Although few of them now live in Fes they are still strongly aware of their origins and most of them return to their native city to marry.

Today, their old family homes in Fes are in a poor state of repair and are often let out as tenements. The population of the old *medina* has soared and the town today shelters some 400,000 people whereas in the past it housed 100,000. Already at the turn of the century Walter Harris had remarked on its echoes of former prosperity and the existing state of decay. 'There is scarcely a glimpse of Fez that is not beautiful, scarcely a glimpse that is not sad,' he reflected, capturing to perfection the city as we see it today.

Still, the faces which pass in the streets of the old town are those of the population which has made Fes, over the centuries, different from other Moroccan towns. The children playing in

In the old town of Fes

the street are often fair-haired, occasionally blue-eyed. Descendants of the refugees from Spain, they have the blood of varied ancestors in their veins. They speak in an Arabic which is somewhat different, more classical, a version which had been preserved in the sophisticated muslim courts of Andalusia.

This population of heterogeneous origin, Jew and Muslim, refugees from Tunisia and Spain, blended to form a composite city with a definite character of its own and tough in the defence of property and rights. The citizens of Fes were hated yet respected by Moulay Ismail, that most powerful of Moroccan Sultans, for they had dared to defy him and had, on occasion, shut their gates to him. Tired of dealing with so stalwart a people he chose to make his own capital in the nearby city of Meknes where, according to Leo Africanus, the people were brave and well mannered but of somewhat limited intelligence; they had always hated the Fasis.

Meknes

Sited on the crest of rolling hills, sixty kilometres west of Fes, Meknes too follows the tradition of historic Moroccan towns with a walled *medina* on one hillside and a broad-avenued new town on another. The old town dates back to the eleventh century and presents a maze of narrow lanes lined with the little stalls of craftsmen and cloth merchants, recalling those of Fes though far less extensive. A few monuments date back to the medieval period, notably the beautiful *medersa* of Bou Inania built by the same Sultan as the *medersa* of the same name in Fes.

It is for the monuments of a far later period, however, that most visitors make for Meknes. Here Moulay Ismail spent his fifty-five year reign building with frenetic energy. Having eschewed the great city of Fes, with its unfortunately independent citizens and the rival capital of Marrakesh, which had been the seat of his predecessors, he was determined that his new capital should lack nothing of the splendour of the other cities. From a purely practical point of view, also, a population kept constantly occupied on massive constructions would have less time and energy to cause trouble.

The 1000-acre ruins of his palace complex are surrounded by truly massive golden walls. Thomas Pellow told how, when he was a slave there, some 30,000 men and 10,000 mules worked each day to build these walls. They were made of earth and lime, stamped down into wooden moulds some three yards long by three feet deep and the width of the wall. Near the great walls is the mausoleum of the Sultan Moulay Ismail. It is one of the few religious buildings in the land which may be visited by non-Muslims.

Extensive gardens (one of which is now an eighteen-hole golf course) and a large ornamental pool were enclosed inside the walls for the pleasure of the Sultan and his large family. Everything, indeed, was on a vast scale. Beside the pool stand the great vaulted ruins of his grain stores, bay after bay faintly lit by small skylights at the apex of the arches. In some of the bays immensely deep wells were bored; around them a track has been worn in the stone floor by the animals who turned the water-wheels. Behind these stores are others, roofless and yet more ruined, although their huge pillars have, in recent times, been replastered. A little beyond are the ruins of the *Roua*, stables which, it was said, could house 12,000 horses, each in its own stall. Above the stables there had once been another great palace in which Moulay Ismail's harem was housed.

Moulay Ismail took as much trouble with the decoration of his palaces as he did with their construction. To obtain marble, mosaics, fine fountains and woodwork, he demolished the splendid Badi Palace of Marrakesh which had been built only a century before by the Saadian dynasty. The destruction of his predecessors' magnificent handiwork caused Moulay Ismail no great heartsearching. For good measure he walled up their exquisite tombs in Marrakesh, thus firmly consigning them to oblivion (but preserving the tombs perfectly for us). The Badi Palace was not the only quarry exploited in the construction of imperial Meknes; only thirty kilometres away lay the strange, but fruitful, ruins known then as Pharaoh's Castle. Marble columns from that site were used in the palaces of Meknes and are said to adorn the magnificent blue-tiled city gateway, the Bab Mansur. The enigma of Pharaoh's Castle, meanwhile, had in fact been deciphered two centuries before by the indefatigably curious Leo Africanus who commented that he, for one, did not believe the Pharaoh story but rather, from inscriptions he had seen there, felt certain it was Roman.

Volubilis and Moulay Idris

A country road winds over the well-farmed landscape from Meknes to Volubilis. This was Pharaoh's Castle of medieval times. Its ancient name, Oualili, seems to have been inherited by its successor, the neighbouring, purely Arab township now known as Moulay Idris.

Volubilis is not the most spectacular of Roman ruins in North Africa but it must be one of the most appealing. Situated at the point where steep, olive-clad hillsides run out onto a grain-rich plain, the ruins lie open and peaceful between the grey-green leaves above and the golden corn below. This is a town of private houses rather than of prestigious public buildings although it is the latter, especially the Triumphal Arch of Caracalla and the basilica, which are visible from across the plain.

Volubilis must have been a pleasant place in which to live. The wide, paved main street, complete with drain running underneath, was flanked with columned arcades. There were public and private baths (the former not so different from the Arab *hammam* of today), bakers' shops and untold numbers of olive presses. The town was walled only in the late second century AD and it could never have been much of a stronghold.

A large area of private houses has been excavated and stands open to the sky. Except where they have been restored the walls stand about a metre high so that the ground plan is everywhere clear to see. These Roman houses were not unlike the traditional Arab houses in plan. One entered a vestibule and then came into a colonnaded courtyard, often with a pool in the centre and mosaic tiling around it. The rooms opening off these courtyards have, in many cases, their mosaic pavements still in place so that the town presents a regular art gallery of Roman mosaics, featuring mythological scenes, especially the Labours of Hercules (believed to have occurred in Morocco), fishes, wild animals, and simple patterns reminiscent of those on the Berber carpets of today. Some of the courtyards are planted with red geraniums and dark cyprus trees, wild flowers grow from the ruined walls and an occasional lizard or chameleon suns itself on the stones. I once watched a sleepy owl blinking in the sunlight on the walls of a former palace.

A series of superb bronze busts and statues, found there, reveal the level of culture in the town. Now housed in the archaeological museum of Rabat they are judged to be among the best bronzes of the entire Roman world. Among them is a superb head of the Berber king, Juba II, whose western capital this may have been, and another of Cato the Elder.

The triumphal arch and the basilica stand far higher and more imposing than the houses, but they have been greatly restored. The grey section of the basilica betrays the part which has always remained upright; the triumphal arch was restored from a ruin. It had not long been in that sorry state however. It fell finally in the great earthquake of 1755 which also destroyed Lisbon and Casablanca. A few years previously the arch had been drawn, in a fairly intact state, by two British officials (John Windus and Captain Henry Boyde) who were on their way to Meknes.

During one visit to Volubilis I gave a lift to a young boy from Moulay Idris who made a precarious living as a guide. The task was more difficult for him than for most since he was completely deaf and dumb. However, Dris was a remarkably intelligent little boy; each time I returned he found me by the number plate on my car and once I had the pleasure of being shown around his home town by him. He pointed out the places of interest, the viewpoints from which tourists liked to take photos, the doors and carvings of artistic value. Somehow he had learned to write his name although there was no way he could pronounce it.

When the Arab prince, Moulay Idris, settled in Morocco, he and his followers made their home on the more readily defensible hillside nearby. Today, a delightfully traditional little Arab town clings to the steep slopes of two adjoining hills; the narrow cobbled streets climb sharply, often in long flights of steps, and the views from one hillside to the other and out over the plain are enchanting. In August of each year the little town is the site of an important pilgrimage which brings visitors from all over

71

The *souq*, Marrakesh

Fes

Tanneries, Fes

Wool dyers' souq, Marrakesh

Wool dyers' souq, Marrakesh

(Jean Luc Soler)

Tanneries, Fes

Roman ruins, Volubilis

Moulay Idris

Medersa Ben Yusuf, Marrakesh

Morocco to the mausoleum of the founder of the Arab state, Moulay Idris I. The vast mausoleum, with its sloping green-tiled roofs, was constructed in the early eighteenth century by the Sultan Moulay Ismail. It provides a splash of colour among the uniformly white-and-beige buildings of the hillside.

Marrakesh

Marrakesh is nearly 500 kilometres south of Fes and Meknes; the distance must often have been appreciated in the past when the cities were contesting the position of the capital of the land. Rival sultans were known to have set out with opposing armies from Fes and Marrakesh to clash in battle somewhere between the two. The road from the northern cities crosses a spur of mountain and then runs through the cultivated plain at the foot of the often snow-capped Atlas. That from Casablanca crosses the same plain, dips to cross the Oum ar Rabia river, then rises to the barren phosphate region of Ben Guerrir. Just before entering Marrakesh the road crosses the Oued Tensift by a bridge built in the twelfth century.

The great walls of Marrakesh rise from the fertile land of the Haouz and above them the minaret of the Koutoubia is visible from miles away across the plain. It seems at first sight an unlikely choice of site for so strategic and frequently assailed a city. Yet the choice was not without purpose: water and food were assured, for the Oued Tensift nurtured a vast palm grove stretching around the north of the town and underground water channels, known here as *foggaras,* ensured the city's needs. Above all, the town dominated the valley outlets which lead to the crucial passes across the High Atlas and thence to the desert beyond. Marrakesh, indeed, looked always to the south, in apprehension of another sortie by turbulent tribes of the desert contesting its power; or eagerly, as the source of trade for the great caravans which periodically left its gates. Old men there can still remember the days when a thousand camels would gather

In the carpet *souq,* Marrakesh

on the square of the Jemaa al Fna for the journey across the Sahara.

For the painter or photographer Marrakesh is one of Morocco's most picturesque cities. It could almost be described in the words, which immortalized Petra, as 'a rose-red city, half as old as time', except that, in Marrakesh, the red mud of which the city is built is closer to terracotta in colour and its age a mere 900 years. Seen in the evening light the walls and buildings glow a deep golden red against the backdrop of snow-capped mountains.

The climate of Marrakesh is extraordinary: throughout the winter the sun shines strong and warm, marred only by a very occasional day when rain and intense cold sweep down from the nearby mountains; in summer it is hot, but only occasionally intolerably hot when a dry wind blows in from the desert. The modern

Churchill at La Mamounia, Marrakesh

hotels are all equipped with attractive swimming pools, often heated in winter, and there most visitors choose to spend the middle of the day.

Strangely, Marrakesh does not exert the immediate attraction of Fes; the impact of that other great medieval city is lacking. Yet its charm is insidious until, finally, one finds it 'has stolen one's heart away'. The warm sunny atmosphere is matched by the gaiety of the people; whereas Fes is dour Marrakesh has much of the cheerfulness associated with black Africa.

Foreigners, who have known Marrakesh, long to return. It became the favourite holiday spot of Sir Winston Churchill during and after the Second World War. He used to stay in the luxurious Mamounia Hotel where a Churchill suite of rooms has been carefully preserved and may be visited today. It is said that he painted his only wartime picture in Marrakesh, but the ones in his rooms are by other members of his family and not his own. More recently, another wartime hero, Field-Marshal Sir Claude Auchinleck, chose to spend his old age there. At the age of ninety-six he still enjoyed a morning stroll in the sun through the tree-lined streets of the new town.

The new town of Marrakesh, built largely by the French during this century, has certainly a great deal of charm. Its broad streets are lined with trees, either orange trees, which fill the streets with their heavy scent when in bloom and add a dramatic splash of colour when the fruit is ripe, or jacarandas which should be seen in May when they are covered with a dense haze of lavender-blue flowers.

By regulation the buildings of the new town are painted the same terracotta colour which the natural mud gives to the old town. Most of the modern hotels are clustered in this district, just outside the old city walls, although a few, such as the Mamounia, are inside the walls. Hotels and restaurants spread their tables and chairs onto the wide pavements and customers sit in the sun enjoying their coffee or freshly-pressed orange juice and watching the world go by.

The massive walls of the city are one of its attractions. Today they are well maintained for the pleasure of visitors; in the past they were constantly patched for the protection of the city. Important visitors were given an impressive reception outside the walls before being escorted in to meet the Sultan. On one diplomatic mission Sir John Drummond Hay was aware, even before seeing the monarch, that relations had cooled for he was greeted by only eighty instead of the usual 3000 horsemen. Walter Harris, accompanying another British mission to the Sultan in Marrakesh, described how they were greeted by the tribesmen, dubious of their sovereign's good sense in receiving such foreigners: 'Compliments flowed as fast as mountain streams – happy in their wording, sonorous in their utterance, and absolutely insincere.'

When James Jackson visited the town nearly two centuries ago he remarked that the walls had been recently repaired to withstand a siege. The town within the walls, on the other hand, was 'quite a heap of ruins', from that and countless other attacks. 'Latterly, however, it has been much depopulated, and owing to the devastations of succeeding conquerors, retains little of its ancient magnificence,' he explained. The situation was not new; three centuries earlier Leo Africanus noted that, although Marrakesh was one of the world's leading cities, it was, in his time, only one third inhabited; there were but five students in the college which had once been a centre of intellectual life and, of the 100 booksellers who had kept their stalls at the foot of the Koutoubia, none then remained. The town reached perhaps its lowest ebb in the latter part of the last century when a team of botanists from Kew found it in a 'ruinous state' and 'utterly repulsive'. Happily, since that time the city's fortunes have soared, its old buildings have been renovated and restored and an air of prosperity prevails.

Some of the architectural monuments are very fine. The Koutoubia minaret, visible from so far out over the plain, is undoubtedly the outstanding example of medieval architecture in the city. It was completed in the late twelfth century by the same Sultan, Yakub al Mansur, who was responsible for the Giralda in Seville and the Tour Hassan in Rabat. The Koutoubia derives its name from the booksellers *(kutubiyin* in Arabic), who once worked at its base. It is decorated with delicate arches and relief patterns in stonework and, around the top, is a band of green-and-white glazed tiles. A sloping ramp inside leads up to the apex which is crowned with three golden globes. Many stories are told about these globes, said to have been donated by Yakub's wife, who gave her jewels to buy them and to be magically protected from theft. Thomas Pellow, who was in Marrakesh 260 years ago as captain of a troop of the Sultan's soldiers, was sceptical of the tale that the tower trembled to deter robbers. He went one night with some companions but, when they had nearly reached the top, there was a great rumbling noise, the tower shook and their lights went out. They fled in terror down the ramp.

Today, at the foot of the Koutoubia, the Cheshire Homes run a home for crippled boys in a charming old house, provided by the Moroccan authorities, which is part of the mosque complex. A dedicated team of young people from several countries look after these boys, teaching them craftwork and how to cope with life for themselves, after they return from the nearby local school. With their crutches or wheelchairs the boys can often be seen, enjoying the sun and the view of life at the heart of the city, even though they cannot get about much. Many of the big hotels offer them a dish of food each week.

On the northern side of the Koutoubia lies the main square of the Jemaa al Fna where the life of the city is at its most pulsating. The square pro-

A snake charmer

vides a great open-air circus where, from morning to evening, entertainers seek to amuse the crowds come in from the countryside or living in the city. Storytellers always draw the largest circle of passionately attentive listeners; they act the parts they tell, aided often by background music of flute, tambourine or drum. A similar accompaniment encourages the Gnaoua dancers who stress the beat with a kind of double-ended metal castanet and swirl the tassels on their cowrie-encrusted black caps.

Snake charmers pull out their slithering charges from under the tambourines, where they are trapped, and encourage them to rear and sway to the sound of their flutes, or entwine them around their own necks or those of any hardy onlookers. Monkey trainers put their sad little monkeys through a series of leaps and somersaults, while the baby monkeys jump unconcerned around the boxes to which they are chained. Spell makers grind up their unlikely ingredients into effective powders, letter writers

pen a quick note for those who have had no schooling, shooting booths offer a chance for the young men to show their skill. At evening time the square throngs with life, the stalls around it light their paraffin lamps and the air throbs with the rhythms of Arabia and of Africa. This is no show put on for the tourist although foreigners are eagerly greeted by the entertainers who hope for a bigger tip; a century ago Joseph Thompson described exactly the same performances as one sees today and he and his companion were the only foreigners in the audience.

North of the square run the narrow, covered alleys of the souq. Here rows of little stalls sell the same goods as their neighbours: henna, nuts and spices; clothing materials, gowns and jellabas; sandals and babouches; bags, belts and leather goods of all kinds; pottery, baskets and woodwork. So much is offered for sale that one wonders it can ever find a buyer. Yet the lanes are packed with a moving stream of humanity and it is strangely stimulating (for those who do not feel claustrophobia) to drift along, part of this dense and continuous throng.

One or two corners of the souq deserve special mention. The little lane off to the right, with the spice stalls, leads into a small square where the stalls also sell dried-up chameleons, dead owls, gazelle horns and jackals' feet. These macabre articles can be ground up to make spells or used in traditional medicines (the dried chameleons are used as an antidote to snake bite); occasionally, one can also find live chameleons in these stalls for they are much in demand by housewives in summer as a rapid remedy against flies.

Beyond these stalls an archway leads through to the attractive alleys of the carpet souq where old and new carpets from the Atlas and beyond are stacked from floor to ceiling in the rows of little shops. Back on the other side of the main alley is another archway which leads to a little square, covered with the spreading branches of a huge old vine. Around the square are the stalls of antique dealers where one may find old

Saadian tombs

school boards, with their beautifully written Koranic texts, ornately carved wooden plaques which supported the camel litters of nomad women in the Sahara, and pieces of old painted furniture. Beyond this the alley narrows and hung across it are bamboo poles supporting skeins of brilliantly coloured wools and silks, for this is the dyers' *souq* with its great metal vats and rainbow colours.

Deep in the heart of the *souq* is an open space around the green-roofed mosque of Ali ben Yusuf which was rebuilt at the beginning of the last century. It stands on a very old site, however, for in front of the mosque is a small domed *kubba* which once stood in the courtyard of an older mosque. This is the oldest building in Marrakesh, built by the Almoravids in the early twelfth century. Although it is two storeys high only the top of the dome appears above ground level, so much has the land risen with the debris of buildings over the centuries. It was only discovered in 1947. It is now surrounded by a high wall and you must go inside and peer up into the

dome to see the delicacy of its decoration, the intricacy of its construction of a shell within a shell. It covers a pool, the ablutions pool of the first mosque to stand there.

By the corner of the mosque a great doorway, under an arch spanning the lane, leads into the *medersa* ben Yusuf. This is a beautiful old college, built in the sixteenth century on the site of an older building and similar to the colleges in Fes. Its central courtyard has a large pool in which the mosaic wall tiles in blue, green, brown, black and white are reflected. Above the tiles the walls are richly decorated with sculpted stucco work and carved cedar wood, the whole capped with curved green tiles. The students' rooms on the upper floor are built around a series of small courtyards which serve as light wells; a balustrade, with carved cedar pillars, runs around each well. In the prayer hall at the eastern end of the main courtyard is a *mihrab* (prayer niche) whose domed ceiling is hung with stucco stalactites.

The Saadian kings who rebuilt this *medersa* left another beautiful memorial: a group of tomb chambers set around a little courtyard. The tombs were walled up by Moulay Ismail and only rediscovered in 1917 when an entrance to them was made through the great walls surrounding both them and the adjoining mosque. A tunnel-like passageway runs between these high walls, hung with a pink-flowered creeper, and opens suddenly into the light of the beautifully kept little garden, planted with rosemary, roses, strong-scented datura and date palms.

This is one of the most beautiful and touching monuments in Morocco and to appreciate its charm one must visit the little garden when it is not full of groups of tourists being hurried through. In the two elegant buildings, arranged in three rooms, simple triangular marble capstones (the shape of chocolate blocks of Toblerone) mark the resting places of kings and princes and of the numerous children of the family who died young. Similar stones set in the garden mark the graves of others. Moorish architecture reached its point of greatest refinement in the traditional decoration of these tombs with their glazed mosaic tiles, fine stucco work carved into honeycombed stalactites at the archways and corners, delicate columns of Italian marble and carved cedar wood.

Not far away are the ruins of the Badi Palace, home of the Saadian kings and famed in its day as the most luxurious palace in Africa. Today, only its shell remains for the rich decoration of its rooms and courts was stripped to furnish the palaces of Meknes. Its massive mud walls, crowned with storks' nests, tower above the large main courtyard planted with orange trees and watered from wide oblong pools. This courtyard is the setting, once a year in early June, of the justly famed Folklore Festival of Marrakesh. A well-directed and beautifully lighted evening performance is given by the leading groups of dancers, acrobats and musicians from all over Morocco, the whole

Folklore festival in Badi Palace (ONMT)

produced as a dramatic show set around some such theme as a marriage or a circumcision celebration. As a climax to the performance mounted horsemen wheel their chargers and fire long rifles in the air, a bonfire is lit and the storks fly, startled and protesting, from their nests.

But a short walk from the Badi Palace lies the Bahia Palace, built by the Sultan's chief minister, Bou Ahmad, at the end of the last century; it is an example of the decoration and comfort of a wealthy residence of traditional Morocco. A series of decorative garden rooms run around an attractive main courtyard and the various wings of the palace are set around other little courts.

Between the two palaces lies the rabbit-warren of alleys of the *mellah,* the Jewish quarter. A hundred years ago Thompson estimated that a third of the population of Marrakesh was Jews. Today, rather fewer remain in the little shops of the *mellah,* some of which are so minute that they are hardly more than cupboards, set some way up in the wall and in which their owners can only sit cross-legged.

Marrakesh is well organized to make one's visit comfortable. At the end of most walks there is a café with tables on the pavement or on a terrace, offering fresh-pressed orange juice to revive the weary. Throughout the town there are horse-drawn carriages ready to transport you, at a gentle pace, through the narrow alleys and out to the cool olive gardens of the Menara or the Aguedal which are one of the pleasures of the place. These ancient gardens are both laid out around huge ornamental pools which serve also for irrigation. In the Menara a charming little pavilion beside the pool has been converted into a small museum. Its thick walls and northern orientation ensure a cool interior, even on the hottest of days. In the summer, local families and visitors come out to relax in the shade and take a picnic under the olive branches.

Girl dressed for her wedding (ONMT)

5 Religion and Tradition

It is in her ancient cities that you feel most strongly the influence of Islam whose importance in Morocco has been strengthened through centuries of proximity with, and struggle against, Christianity. Although Muslims and Christians worship the same God and revere many of the same prophets they have been, over the centuries, committed opponents. Today the feeling of animosity has abated as both peoples have seen a greater threat in the spread of communism and the denial of God. Westerners are welcomed in Morocco where considerable efforts are made to make them feel at home.

This has required some adaptation on the part of the Moroccans. Traditionally Muslims are very modestly dressed, especially the women who, in the past, were always covered from head to foot. An English traveller to Morocco in the last century remarked that the Moroccans were shocked to see a man wearing trousers. Today many of them wear trousers themselves but they still feel that it is unseemly for a man to walk in the streets of the city in shorts, and even more so for a woman to wear shorts or a very short skirt.

Their mosques they reserve to themselves as places of worship and non-Muslims are not allowed to enter. On the other hand, they readily allow freedom of worship to other religions and there are both christian churches and jewish synagogues throughout the land.

Jews have lived in Morocco from the earliest times, some having sought refuge there perhaps as early as the time of the destruction of the temple in Jerusalem. These original Jews live in communities throughout the countryside and are often Berber speaking. Some indeed may be the descendants of Berber tribes converted to Judaism, possibly even before the Romans introduced Christianity. Others, the more sophisticated, came as refugees from Spain. They settled in the cities and brought advanced skills with them. Their services were useful to the sultans who gave them protection. The Jewish quarters of Moroccan cities are always sited close by the king's palace.

During the centuries there were times when the situation of the Jews deteriorated and they were oppressed (though never to anything even approaching the extent to which they were in Europe in the mid-twentieth century). Their districts were called *mellahs* (from *milh* meaning salt) because they had the unpleasant duty of salting the severed heads of rebels for exposure on the city gates – less unpleasant though, one would say, than it was for the Muslims whose heads were being salted. The Jews were not allowed to defend themselves (except in their own homes); they were abused in the streets and were often the first victims when the tribes attacked the towns. In 1863 a British envoy, Sir Moses Montefiore, travelled through Morocco to inspect the condition of his fellow religionaries and to request favourable treatment for them from the Sultan; a century and a half earlier a Moroccan envoy to London had demanded just treatment for the Moroccan Jews who lived and traded in Gibraltar.

Today the majority of the Moroccan Jewish community, which once numbered nearly 300,000, have left Morocco. Those who have stayed on live in peace, as poor peasants in the country, or rich merchants in the city, or any-where between the two. The *mellahs* have been abandoned and most city Jews have settled in the modern districts. Those who have emigrated retain a love for their native land which is illustrated by a story told by a Palestinian settled in Morocco. He wished to visit his family in Israel but was held up at the frontier and not allowed in. He sat in fear all day. In the evening an Israeli soldier came to question him: 'Why had he come? Where was he from?' 'Casablanca,' he replied. Suddenly the atmosphere changed; the soldier threw his arms about his neck. He himself was a Jew from Casablanca. How was such and such a street? And was his family's old shop still there? The doors were open and the other exile, the Palestinian, walked through to rejoin his family.

For the Muslims of Morocco religious festivals are of great importance. Ramadan, the fasting month, is taken as seriously in Morocco as it is in Mecca, the people abstaining from food, cigarettes or water (and the latter is the hardest sacrifice in a hot country) from sunrise to sunset. Lancelot Addison, an Englishman who lived in Morocco in the seventeenth century, recorded that a breach of the daylight fast was punished by stoning to death. Today penalties are less extreme, but to drink or smoke in the street could still bring a Moroccan into trouble with the authorities. Throughout the land the people watch for the sun to drop below the horizon and only then, with a sigh of relief, sit down to break their fast with a cup of milky coffee, and a sticky cake rolled in honey or syrup. They follow this with a bowl of *harira,* a nourishing meat and vegetable soup, also accompanied by sticky cakes or dates.

All families eat more and better during Ramadan, than at other times, for their appetites are sharpened by a long day's work with no break. People stay up eating, then they stroll around the streets where the shops stay open especially late, until after midnight. This is a colourful, elated scene; people feel united in their daytime suffering and night-time enjoyment so that for many Ramadan is, despite it all, the happiest month of the year.

The other great muslim festival which is eagerly celebrated is the Eid al Kabir which comes at the end of the *hajj,* the pilgrimage to Mecca. All Muslims are enjoined to make the pilgrimage once in a lifetime if they have the means so to do, and there have always been Moroccans among the pilgrims, despite the distance they have to travel. Today, with air travel, the journey is much easier and the airport at Casablanca is crowded for weeks on end before and after the pilgrimage. Muslims who have made the pilgrimage may use the title *al hajj* and they are often referred to simply by that title. At the end of their pilgrimage the pilgrims at Mecca sacrifice a sheep, in memory of Abraham's sacrifice of a sheep in place of his son. At home in Morocco every family, rich and poor, tries to obtain a sheep to kill and for a day or two they feast on the meat. For weeks afterwards strips of meat hang from clothes lines or any other suitable spot, drying in the sun. In some country districts, during the days following the feasts, men dress up in the sheep skins, blacken their faces, and pursue their neighbours, flailing them in jest with other skins.

Local festivals are also of great importance, especially in the countryside. Every little village has a local saint whom the people revere and whose burial place is usually marked with a *kubba,* a small white-domed shrine. The saint was usually some particularly holy man, often a *shereef,* who had lived in the district and spread his *baraka* there in the past. His shrine is a place of prayer and pilgrimage, often surrounded by a cemetery and protected trees reminiscent of a sacred grove.

At the shrines of the most important regional saints an annual festival is held. These festivals are known as *moussems* and combine devotion, commerce and entertainment in a manner which recalls the fairs of medieval Europe. On the open ground beside the shrine a great number of

It is a Muslim's duty to give alms

83

Caidal tent

Fantasia riders (ONMT)

tents are erected. Around the outside are the black tents of the semi-nomads who will camp there. Then there are simple white tents or shelters which serve as booths for the display of goods to be sold and these are often set up in rows like the streets of a village. Towering here

and there above the others are the tall, circular, white *caidal* tents with their rows of black, chessboard-figure patterns and pointed roofs. With their bright-coloured interior linings they look for all the world like tents from a medieval tournament or battle field. They will house the

84

local notables or provide a place for eating and drinking.

In the evening there will be music and dancing groups and a dozen stalls will offer hot bread straight from the oven, sizzling *beignets,* steaming *kebabs* to eat in one's fingers, while more ambitious stalls make *couscous* or chicken. Highlight of the *moussem* is always the *fantasia,* held in the late afternoon as the heat of the day wanes. Teams of horse-men, magnificently mounted and caparisoned, gather at one end of a long open space. At a sign the horses of the first team stop prancing on the spot to dash forward in a fast gallop, their riders throwing up their long rifles in the air. As they reach the end of the ride all must fire their rifles at the same moment in the air and rein in their mounts to a crashing halt. It is the precision with which they carry out these two manoeuvres that determines the winning team.

The major events in the life of a family are also marked with religious ritual. When there is a death, friends and relatives gather at the house of the bereaved and continue to visit during the customary forty days' mourning period. In the country the body is simply carried on an open bier to the cemetery, a field lying close to the village, where it is laid to rest in a grave marked by two stones set on end. In the city the cemeteries have been removed to the periphery.

In the life of a boy the first festival, of which he is aware, is that of his circumcision. This is carried out at the age of eight years for the first born (especially in families from Fes, sometimes earlier in other places) and earlier for younger brothers who are often all circumcised together. It is the occasion for a large family reunion when the boys who have been circumcised are dressed in traditional white robes and may be carried round on a large platter supported on the shoulders of female domestics who move rhythmically, making the high pitched *youyou* cries which Moroccan women use to express ritual joy.

Marriage, the decisive event in any life, is also the most important family festival. It is the occasion of a great feast which may last for three days; friends and relatives will spend the night eating and being entertained by musicians and possibly dancers. The open carts of the poor people, decked with ribbons and carrying the gifts, parade through the streets, accompanied by men blowing trumpets, to announce the wedding. The homes of richer folk are hung with electric lightbulbs for the occasion, and the wedding procession may drive through the streets late at night, their horns blaring joyfully (though less to the joy of sleeping neighbours).

Traditionally, receptions for men and women guests are held separately, although nowadays many families hold mixed receptions, and some give both on different days. Where separate receptions are held the groom arrives late in the evening at the women's reception to carry off his bride to his parents' home. She is dressed in oriental splendour, her long, brightly coloured under-gown covered with a transparent over-gown embroidered in gold thread, forming a train behind her. She may be so loaded down with heavy silver jewellery, hanging especially across her forehead and down either side of her cheeks, that she can scarcely move. But this is of little consequence for she is not meant to move but to sit like some quaint doll, her skirts held out around her by stuffing with cushions, her hands and feet decorated with intricate patterns of henna, until the moment should come for her husband to take her to her new life.

In the past, marriages were always arranged, often with a cousin or some close relative. The bride might not see her husband before her wedding day. Her parents chose for her. Today in the towns this custom is being abandoned for the girls are freer than they have ever been. Many go to school or college with the boys or meet them on the way home from school or the office. Many boys of influential families, who go abroad to study, have learnt there to demand a wife whose company they can enjoy – in spite of the opposition which they may get from their parents.

In the countryside the Berber villagers were always freer for the girls and women work in the fields along with the men and for the most part go unveiled. They were often able to find a mate to their liking. A country girl's first marriage, however, is usually arranged by her family. Country people think that around thirteen is the best and safest age at which to marry their daughters, although the official age is fifteen. These marriages are often arranged more with an eye to securing the family property (of which girls inherit half as large a share as boys and so are frequently married to a boy cousin) than with concern for the girl's happiness. They often end in early divorce, after which the divorced girl has more freedom and a greater chance to choose her next husband.

The change in marriage customs, especially in the towns, is indicative of the change which is spreading across Morocco in the lives of the women on whom, over the centuries, Islam has lain heaviest. The Koran allows a man to have four wives providing he can treat them all equally; the woman's life was restricted to the home.

Today, education and the influence of western ways is rapidly altering family life, at least in the city. Few men have more than one wife and those who do come either from the very highest levels of society, where expense is no constraint, or from the lowest, where they have nothing to lose. In the upper-middle classes, at least, marriages now seem to be stable and long-lasting. Women get out and about more and many veiled mothers are accompanied in the streets by daughters dressed in blue jeans and fashionable sweaters. When they leave school these girls continue to wear western dress; very large numbers work in shops or offices or as teachers; or they may continue their studies in Morocco, France or even Russia or the United States. I have met Moroccan women who are practising doctors, anaesthetists, chemists, psychiatrists, barristers, diplomats, archaeologists, painters and journalists, who are senior officials in banks or who run their own businesses. Of course they are in the minority in Morocco, as such women are still in the west, and many Moroccan women feel that they have been frustrated by family or social restrictions and have not had the opportunity to fulfil themselves. Nevertheless, it seems that for families who are willing for their girls to play a full role in society, the doors are now open. Even girls from poor families can continue their education to the top if their family can support them (though that is the big prob-

lem). There are plenty of young Moroccan women able and determined to take advantage of these opportunities.

The lead in the emancipation of women was given in Morocco from above. Their greatly loved and respected King Muhammad v was determined, after independence, that women as well as men should share in the development of their country. He gave his daughters a modern education and, as early as 1943, encouraged them to appear unveiled in public and to play a part in national affairs. Their lead was followed by girls in the cities throughout the land. Visitors to Morocco today, coming back to the country after several years' absence, are invariably surprised by the modern appearance of the girls in the city streets, and by the relaxed way in which groups of boys and girls walk along together. 'Twenty years ago you would never have seen such a thing,' an elderly English inhabitant remarked.

For the married woman the birth of her first child is tremendously significant. In a land where, until very recently, women have had no other role than that of wife and mother, and where infant mortality was high, the birth of many children was a woman's greatest desire. To produce no child at all was, and still is, a major tragedy. Since fertility pills have not yet reached the ordinary Moroccan woman (although contraceptive pills are doing so), her sole recourse is to magic. She will pray at a shrine known for its *baraka* and leave shreds of her clothing hanging there, or on a sacred tree. She may try even more symbolic magic, feeding hard-boiled eggs to fish or to the eels which live in such sacred pools as the one at the Chellah in Rabat. Especially when a boy is born there is great rejoicing in the family and a feast may be given. The family will be entertained again seven days later when the baby is named. A baby is thought particularly vulnerable to wicked spirits, and especially to the Evil Eye. The mother will stay at home for several days, before the birth, to avoid the Evil Eye, protected

Gnaoua dancers (ONMT)

by such charms and magic as she can obtain.
The design of a hand, the Hand of Fatima, is
thought a strong protection against the Evil Eye;
it is painted on walls, worn as jewellery, painted

today on lorries and cars.

The baby himself will wear lockets containing
charms or passages from the Koran, protective
beads and earrings as a protection against evil

A *kubba*, country shrine

a. Azemmour b. Essaouira

Tour Hassan, Rabat, from the mausoleum of King Muhammad V

Socco Grande, Tangier

spirits. One should never praise a young child nor say how pretty he is, for fear of attracting the Evil Eye to him, and it is customary to add, 'Poor thing' and 'May God preserve them' when speaking to a mother of her children. When the child's hair grows, especially in Berber areas in the countryside, it may be shaved leaving only one long lock, a tuft by which his guardian angel may seize him to pull him out of danger. Despite these precautions many children still die young and families tend to produce many babies, to be on the safe side.

While the birth of no child within a marriage can be tragic, the birth of a child outside wedlock is almost certainly more so. Islamic society is particularly jealous of the honour of its women and an illegitimate child can be a disaster. Berber society adapted to this stringent ruling with the convenient belief in 'the child asleep in its mother's womb'. If the husband goes away for several years, as often happens in the Moroccan countryside where men must leave to seek a living in the city or even in France, a child born during his departure will be accepted by father and neighbours alike as having been asleep in the womb. In the Berber tribe of the Ait Haddidou, where young people frequently divorce, the period during which a child may be asleep in its mother's womb is fixed as two years; providing the mother, on divorcing, declares that she is pregnant of a sleeping child, any baby born will be accepted as legitimate within that time limit.

The most widespread belief in the supernatural, in Morocco as throughout Islamic countries, is the belief in spirits, *jinns* (the 'genies' of the *Arabian Nights* stories). For the simple people their world is populated by a host of *jinns*, good and bad, whose activities and interventions in human life serve to explain the otherwise inexplicable. In Arabia an Englishman who stayed in a remote village recounted that his hosts were anxious when he wanted to go out for a walk at dawn: 'If any man, animal or other creature should call you by your name, on no account must you answer. It is certain to be a *jinn*,' they warned. Moroccan villagers might easily express identical sentiments.

Jinns can possess people, it is believed. Their possession might be for the person's good, bringing a cure for illness or healing a wound. Or it might be to his harm, causing illness or even madness. Some troupes of dancers, such as the dark-skinned Gnaoua who, with their cowrie-covered hats with swirling tassels, work as professional dancers throughout the land, are thought in their more frantic dances to perform when possessed by spirits.

One day Hassan, the gardener, did not appear for work. A few days later a small boy on an old bicycle arrived at the gate: 'Hassan is very ill, please come,' was his message. We followed him to an extensive shanty town on the edge of the city. The shacks, built of boards and corrugated iron, were set in neat rows and some of their inhabitants were even then sweeping the dusty alley before their doors.

As we approached Hassan's shack we were aware that something was amiss. His shack was prettier than the others thanks to a huge grapevine growing by the door and over the roof. Later in the year he brought us a basket filled with delicious grapes as an offering from his vine. On this summer morning, however, a crowd of neighbours was gathered around his door and in the small front room which served as a kitchen.

In the back room, on a bed by the wall, Hassan lay looking very ill. 'What is the matter?' we asked anxiously. 'Ah, the *jinns* have got me,' he replied sadly. 'Each year at this time, just before Ramadan, they seize me. You remember last year.' I did indeed remember that, last summer, he had been ill and had trekked many kilometres out of town to a shrine known for its healing powers. 'We must go to a doctor,' we urged, but he refused, afraid at our suggestion. 'That would anger the *jinns* and it would be worse.'

We did our best to determine what might be wrong. He had acute pains in all his joints, perhaps rheumatism from the extreme humidity

Spell shop in the *souq* (Jean-Luc Soler)

of summer on the sea coast. We left him a small bottle of aspirin to alleviate the pain, in the hopes that the *jinns* would not notice it. But he preferred to continue with his own cure of spells to placate the *jinns* and *kif* to deaden the pain. In the end it came to the same thing; he was back at work the next week, the *jinns*/rheumatism had left him. In his case it had made no difference whether he believed his illness to be the work of *jinns,* or of a malady whose name would be even more of a frightening mystery to him.

The people do the best they can to control this invisible, unpredictable world around them, using age-old methods culled from the ancient

and keep away evil. Protective symbols with well-tried powers of good are wrought into jewellery, woven into mats, painted on walls: of such are the ubiquitous Hand of Fatima and the six-pointed star, the Seal of Solomon, a symbol used in ceremonial rites throughout the world and indeed the symbol of the Kingdom of Morocco itself, woven in green on a red background in the country's flag.

The Evil Eye, which can cause sickness and death, is thought to be cast by humans as well as other agents such as the camera. It can be turned aside by the five-finger symbol, the Hand of Fatima, and by striking objects which may attract the eye to themselves. A donkey's skull propped up on a stick in the garden, an old cooking pot or a pair of goat's horns on the roof, eye-shaped objects such as the huge red lozenge woven into the back of the black Atlas cloaks, or lion's claws or shark's teeth may all serve to avert the ever-present menace.

Beyond this there are spells and potions which can be mixed and here one moves into a world more African than Eastern. In the *souqs* of the old *medinas* rows of tiny shops sell an intimidating assortment of grisly bric-a-brac which the knowledgeable can grind together to produce a mixture bound to bring back a recalcitrant lover, discomfit an enemy or turn aside the Evil Eye.

folk-knowledge of the Middle East and Africa. Beneath the powerful, ever-present flow of Islam in their lives runs a deeper, more ancient current to which they resort in case of need, alongside their orthodox daily prayers.

Incense, of Java wood, amber, musk and storax, is burned extensively to purify the air

Rif women in Tetuan (ONMT)

6 The Sea Coast

Hundreds of miles of golden beaches and a deep blue sea, sparkling with white crests of breaking surf, are one of the great delights of Morocco. You can enjoy the different attributes of two seas, the Mediterranean on the one side and the Atlantic on the other, especially if you stay in Tangier set, as it is, strategically at the junction of the two. To the south of the town are endless stretches of undisturbed, apparently untrodden sand which are characteristic of the Atlantic shore; to the east are rocky coves with their sheltered crescents of sand which are typical of the Mediterranean where the Rif mountains rise straight from the sea.

Much of the Mediterranean shore is unexploited and largely inaccessible because of the steep mountains and lack of a coastal road. Even where the road does follow the coast, between Tangier and Ceuta, it rarely comes down to the beach. From Tetuan to Ceuta, however, the coastline is lower and easier of access and a series of holiday villages – Cabo Negro, M'diq, Restinga, Smir – have been built in bright modern styles. New white-painted chalets and apartments rise straight from the beach and the boats of the local fishermen pull in below them. The thatched-roof shelters of Club Méditerranée villages are dotted along some of these beaches.

The Atlantic coastline, on the contrary, is hugged for most of its length by a good asphalt road, some stretches of which give magnificent views of sandy beaches (south of Tangier), of ancient raised beaches and cliffs (from Al Jadida to Safi), and of mountains dropping to the sea (north of Agadir). You can easily spend a whole day on an open beach with no other company but that of the flocks of sea birds who seem to spend their life standing patiently at the water's edge in the hope of seizing some shell-fish washed up by the waves.

Such a coastline is ideal for water sports although the undertow can be strong and the sea dangerous when the tide is going down. You can swim all the year round, surfing attracts enthusiasts especially to the beaches north of Agadir for the three winter months, sailing boats set out to sea from all the little harbours and wind surfing and water skiing are the latest fashion in harbours and sheltered bays, as well as on the inland mountain lakes.

All along the coast are the ancient walled towns which protected Morocco's little harbours over the centuries. Many of them are of extremely ancient origin, founded by the Phoenicians centuries before the time of Christ and often developed in later times by the Romans. Their massive fortifications date from the troubled centuries of strife between Morocco and Spain and Portugal. These sea ports were Morocco's windows to the outside world, the only places where foreigners penetrated freely; the contact was not always easy and comfortable as the old cannon on the great walls and towers show.

The fortunes of the little harbours rose and fell, as a result of the agricultural success of the hinterland providing exports, or of the movements of the court and capital city. Most of the ports enjoyed a period of predominance and prosperity, at one time or another, until the present century when Casablanca seems to have ousted all rivals.

Arrival of a fishing boat

Migrations of the shoals of fish, which feed the fishing fleets, also affect the prosperity of the old harbour towns. The people of the sea coast have always been dependent on fish for much of their sustenance. Layers of shells are found in the debris of the many large caves hollowed into the old cliff line, just inland of the present shore, and in which extremely ancient human remains have also been found. On the dunes, to the south of Agadir, flint tools mixed with whale bones show where, in the Stone Age, a group of people camped for a while to feast on a whale washed up on the shore. Indeed, so many whales have been washed up on the beach there, at the Oued Massa, that the place has been linked with the story of Jonah and it is claimed

(Moroccan sardines and tinned tunny fish are well known), salted, or dried for animal food. In the southern suburbs of Safi large sardine plants make their presence known by the smell of dried fish.

Fresh fish are just as noticeable all along the sea shores. By the road side men and boys hold up large fish, or bundles of small ones, to attract the custom of passing motorists. Fishing boats pull up onto the beaches and, straight away, are surrounded by a crowd of haggling buyers. On the quays of some of the harbours, especially that at Essaouira, sardines are taken from the boats and grilled over charcoal, to be eaten on the spot, accompanied by fresh bread.

The men who sell by the roadside eke a precarious existence, fishing alone with a line from the rocks, or venturing out over the waves in cockle-shell boats. 'I am always afraid that one day I shall not come back from a fishing trip,' remarked Muhammad, recalling the time when his lorry-tyre coracle had punctured some distance out to sea and he had managed, after a long struggle, to swim into shore with the aid of the floats on his nets. At nineteen he was a highly experienced fisherman for he had been the family bread-winner since the age of ten. His father, a policeman, had been killed while directing traffic at an accident; at the time Muhammad and his younger sister Fatima were children. Zohra, their mother, was a woman of strong character and managed to rear the children alone in her little hut on the sea coast. Now Muhammad was a man and Fatima was sixteen. She stayed at home helping her mother and never left the house. Recently, a young man from the town had come to ask for her hand in marriage but Zohra had decided that his family were no good because, she claimed, they drank alcohol. The present of a pullover, which he had brought, was returned, but the sugar, cakes and other foodstuffs had already been eaten. Fatima was regretful; life as a married woman must have seemed to offer more freedom than the

that here he was finally thrown up by the whale.

By Roman times the fishing industry was well developed. Purple dye was extracted from murex shells on the island of Essaouira and large fish-salting vats at Lixus, near Larache, show that the Romans also processed their fish. Today, much of the fish brought into the little fishing harbours is still processed, tinned

confinement of her own three, windowless, small rooms.

Individual fishermen, like Muhammad, make but a tiny contribution to the nation's total haul: all along the coasts open wooden boats go out with their nets, seine netting along the beaches, trawling further out to sea. And from every little harbour fleets of larger fishing boats set out for the horizon. They are not well equipped with cold-store facilities, however, and are dependent on the movements of the fickle shoals; when the sardines are close in to Morocco's Atlantic coasts the fleets from Agadir and Safi come in heavily laden and the ports are prosperous; when the shoals move away there is despair among the fishermen and their neighbours, who work in processing plants, and the men involved in marketing and exporting, and the housewives who find fish has become too expensive for their tables.

Rabat, the Capital City

Rabat is the only city on the coast which ranks as an 'imperial city', a city built to be a capital by the sultans of past centuries, but one which did not, in fact, achieve its destiny until the beginning of the French Protectorate when it finally became the capital of Morocco. Its name goes back to a fortified tenth-century monastery, a

ribat, whose occupants busied themselves with religious struggles. Its form was determined by the twelfth-century Almohad conqueror, Yakub al Mansur, who used it as a base for his campaigns in Spain and who planned to make it his capital. He developed the old *ribat,* already enlarged into a *kasbah* by his grandfather, to create the district known today as the Kasbah of the Oudaia. He built the great line of walls which runs, apparently without purpose, inland from the old *medina* to the royal palace and beyond, and he started construction of the huge mosque of which only the Tour Hassan stands more or less intact. His mosque, like his city, was abandoned after his death and only really came into its own in the present century when the land within the city walls was at last filled with the streets and houses of a capital and the magnificent twelfth-century gateway of Bab Rouah was pressed into service as an art gallery.

Although the larger part of the city of Rabat has been built during this century it is yet a capital city with immense character and charm. The site alone is impressive: the buildings pile on steep cliffs, dropping to the sea on the western side and the river Bou Regreg ('Father of Reflections') on the north. Throughout the spring and summer storks circle lazily above the river; all year round the waves break in white

96

Ruined mosque and Hassan Tower, Rabat (ONMT)

foam on the bar at the river's mouth; across, on the opposite bank, the walls and towers of Salé provide a golden echo to those of the Kasbah of the Oudaia, reassuring, no doubt, in centuries past when foreign warships thundered at the river mouth, only prevented by their deeper draught from entering in pursuit of local craft.

The modern town is well laid out with wide streets shaded by shopping arcades or avenues of trees. These modern boulevards run right down to, but do not penetrate, the walls of the old *medina* beyond which the contrast in town planning is absolute. Here a warren of narrow, traffic-free alleys shelter the small booths and craftsmen's shops of the *souq*. There, in the modern streets, jewellers, dress boutiques, bookshops and furniture stores offer the wares of Europe, Japan and America. The wealthier

97

citizens of the modern town take their relaxation on the golf course which is romantically sited where the Mamora forest creeps up to the very back doorstep of the city. The King, himself, is among the leading enthusiasts of golf. On the other side of the town, on the cliffs above the sea and across the river by the walls of Salé, the people bury their dead, in peaceful seclusion, in cemeteries lapped endlessly by the sound of the waves.

Just such a site was chosen for the mausoleum of the late King, Muhammad v, since the ancient mosque in which it is sited stands also on a cliff, above the Bou Regreg. At one end of the paved courtyard, planted with a forest of broken pillars, which was to have been the mosque, stands the magnificent ochre-coloured Tower of Hassan with its delightfully intricate raised-stone-work decoration. It is the sister tower to the Giralda of Seville and the Koutoubia of Marrakesh and, had it been finished, might have been the greatest of the three. One can climb the ramp inside to command an extensive view over Rabat and Salé from the top. At the other end has been raised the startlingly white pavilion and mosque of the royal mausoleum, decorated with intricate stucco work and capped with green-tiled roofs. The mausoleum may be visited by non-Muslims also: from an interior balcony you look down onto a black marble floor, so shiny it appears covered with water, in the centre of which stands the raised tomb. In a corner of the building an old man sits cross-legged and reads aloud unceasingly from the Koran. Outside, members of the Royal Guard, in their picturesque white cloaks and red uniforms, stand guard on foot or mounted on horseback.

Where the river runs into the sea a high bluff is crowned by the strongly walled Kasbah of the Oudaia. This was the fortress of the Almohads, a base for their wars in Spain; five centuries later it again served as a fortress, this time for the Moorish exiles from Spain who carried on, by sea, their struggle against their christian conquerors. Then Rabat and Salé became pirate strongholds and, for a while, declared themselves an independent Republic of the Bou Regreg. The old iron cannons of these and later battles still adorn the towers and gateways of the walled town.

The main entry to the *kasbah* is through the monumental Oudaia Gate at the head of an impressively wide set of steps. This huge twelfth-century gateway is beautifully decorated with relief carving in ochre-coloured stone. The geometric designs and Koranic inscriptions, which form its major decoration, are enlivened by carefully carved scallop shells and a pair of little eels at the spring of the arch. Within the walls the well-kept narrow streets and white-painted houses create one of Morocco's most attractive *medinas*. The streets climb the steep hillside in wide steps, flowering, climbing plants tumble over courtyard walls, huge pottery urns decorate some of the house terraces. An open platform, perched high above the sea, gives a sudden brilliant view over the sparkling waters of the river mouth and the walls of Salé on the opposite bank.

At the lower corner of the *kasbah* enclosure a shady Andalusian garden has been created within the high old walls. Its cobbled paths and sunken flower beds are always a blaze of colour and offer a welcome retreat from the pace of life in the modern city and the glare of the mid-day sun. Through the garden an archway leads into a little tiled terrace, set on the ramparts, where an open-air café with shady arcades offers welcome mint tea, sweet Moroccan cakes, and a beautiful view of the river and the ramparts of the upper Oudaia. The most romantic entry to the Oudaia is through another archway out of the café, leading to a cobbled lane rising in wide steps into the heart of the old *kasbah*. It has the added advantage of by-passing the groups of boys, who hang around the gateways, demanding to show you around 'before the *kasbah* closes' (at some notional time, always about twenty minutes after the present).

Another beautiful garden has been created

within the old walled site of the Chellah. This great wall, which echoes that of the Oudaia, is dramatically sited on a grassy promontory overlooking the river. Unlike the Oudaia, however, the area within the walls is almost empty of buildings. Yet it is a place with a long and varied past. Walk down the main alleyway between the flowering shrubs and brilliant annual flowers and, suddenly, you stand on a wide terrace overlooking a hillside covered with grey stone ruins. This is the outline of the pre-Roman and Roman town which was known as Sala Colonia (clearly the origin of the name of modern Salé). A forum, the outline of a temple and the foundations of an artisans' quarter are the, at first sight, rather unintelligible remains of this earliest Rabat. It marked the limit of Roman colonization. On the southern outskirts of today's Rabat, where the coast road branches off from the main road to the south, stands the stump of a great rampart and ditch: the *limes,* designed to keep out the 'barbarians' – the threatening Berber tribes, and the herds of rampaging elephants.

Behind the Roman ruins rise others, far higher and built in the golden-ochre stone of the medieval Islamic city. Here is a minaret, crowned with storks' nests and a roofless ruined mosque in whose floor are set the royal tombs of its builders, the Merinid dynasty. A massive fig tree grows out of the ruined wall above the tombs and, through the ruined arches, sunbeams fall on the quiet graves in a pattern of light and shade. Beyond the mosque is an exquisite little garden, its paths lined with orange trees, the splendid, decorative raised-stone-work of the mosque enclosing it on one side, the great golden ramparts forming its wall on the other.

Uphill from the mosque a group of religious buildings are scattered across the hillside: a number of *kubbas,* domed tombs of holy men, a few inscribed tombstones and, beyond them, a pool surrounded by a row of low barrel-vaulted buildings. The waters of the pool run under the buildings and from their shadows emerge the long grey forms of large eels. Now and then a wistful young woman walks down the steps to the water and throws into it a hard-boiled egg which is greedily gobbled by the eels. The symbolism of the act is patent; the hope is fertility. Around the pool families of thin cats and kittens laze in the sun, springing to purring life when they see visitors clutching eggs. Visiting children, and those in the secret, know that eels eat only whites while cats love the yolks, so both can be fed for the price of one egg. While the interior of the Chellah remains empty, with its dreams of the past, the living and dead of Rabat are clustered closely under its walls outside. Huge cemeteries extend above the sacred enclosure; below, shanty towns tumble down the steep hillside to the water's edge.

Inland from the Chellah, through the great wall and into the new town, a longish walk will bring you to the archaeological museum, the one place which can breathe vitality into the ruined grey-stone walls of Roman days, both of the Chellah and of Volubilis. Here are the everyday objects of Roman town life: mirrors, combs, chisels, cooking pots and childrens' toys. Here, also, is the collection of fine bronze sculptures found at Volubilis, some of the world's greatest Roman bronzes. Other galleries of the appealing little museum display objects from the cave dwellings of Paleolithic man, hollowed in the old cliff facing the sea, or rock carvings of the Bronze Age found in the high mountains of the Atlas.

Across the river from Chellah a visit to Salé takes one in a different direction in the timescale. True, its medieval walls and old streets have still an aura of the past, but cars can penetrate into the heart of the old *medina* and, around its central square, shops advertise Kodak films and Coca-Cola. It is even harder to imagine yourself back into the stirring days of the republic of pirates whose very name, the Sallee Rovers, struck terror into the hearts of European seamen, when you look down to the gol-

Modern Casablanca

den beach below with its rows of candy-striped beach huts, for all the world like an Edwardian picture-postcard come to life.

In the centre of the old town a fine fourteenth-century *medersa* reminds you that it was religious strife which brought these pirates into being. Yet the complexity of that troubled past is symbolized in the religious procession for the festival of *Mouloud* when wax images are carried through the streets just as they are in the christian processions in southern Spain.

Casablanca

The businessmen's hotels, the Casablanca, the Mansour and the Marhaba, are clustered within a stone's throw of the central square, Place Mohammed v. This hectic city centre, with its bizarre, coloured dome lighting a pedestrian subway, its acres of tarmac, clusters of traffic lights and nerve-wracking traffic system, leaves its imprint on the visitor staying in one of the big hotels. 'Casablanca is the least Moroccan of any town,' he mutters sadly as he hurries on.

There is nothing in the Place Mohammed v to make him suspect that here the weekly market was held seventy years ago. Nothing to show that the old city wall stood on the south-western corner of the square. He will probably never think of venturing into the little lanes leading in from this corner, into the old *medina* which is still enclosed on two sides by substantial walls. True, this *medina* is far less old than those, say, of Meknes and Fes. Yet its narrow lanes, with their crowded shops and its old sea-gate, do conjure up the spirit of old Morocco; at the beginning of this century, the old *medina* was Casablanca and it was all there was.

The modern town has burst out of the old *medina* like a bubble. First to be built were the elegant tree-lined boulevards of the French town, now all with Moroccan names – Mohammed el Hansali, Moulay Youssef, Hassan II – the wide green space of the Parc de la Ligue Arabe, and the imposing municipal buildings, in Franco-Moorish style, of the Place des Nations Unies.

The Boulevard Mohammed el Hansali is the embodiment of this change: it runs where once ran the *oued,* which brought water to the city, and the city walls which defended the town. It springs from the Place Mohammed V, where at night the city gates would close to the market place outside, and leads to the large modern port, *raison d'être* of today's Casablanca. There, at the turn of the century, small boats pulled up on the beach, and there the killing of nine port-construction workers in 1907 gave French troops the excuse to land in Morocco. This landing in Casablanca turned the tide of centuries and took not just the city itself, but the whole country, out of the Middle Ages and into the twentieth century in one breath-taking leap.

For the French, Casablanca, their first foothold in Morocco, had a special appeal. Each decade saw new districts constructed: the art-nouveau façades of the main shopping streets around Boulevard Mohammed V were elaborately decorated and still house the best and most expensive shops; the new *medina* was built in 'traditional' style with the narrow lanes and

arched gateways of an Arab town and the arcades of some latter-day Annecy; it is, perhaps, the best place in Morocco to bargain for Moroccan garments and handcrafts. Maarif

In the town centre, Casablanca

was built on a grid plan of ruler-straight lines for the poor Europeans; Spanish is still spoken more widely than French in its streets and the stall-holders in the market, many of whom cannot write down your account, converse happily in French, Spanish and Arabic. Today, they are taking, with relief, to pocket computers, to solve the horrible arithmetic of 75 francs worth of potatoes, 365 of artichokes, 420 worth of avocados, and so on.

Further out, to the south and west, the creation of garden suburbs transformed a treeless waste which had depressed earlier travellers: 'A less attractive spot than Casablanca it is difficult to imagine,' wrote Joseph Hooker and John Ball in 1878. 'Not a tree gives variety to the outline or shelter from the blazing sun. The attempts made by the residents to cultivate the orange and other useful trees have met with little success. The eye seeks in vain the gay shrubs . . . of the Mediterranean.' Today, these suburbs more closely resemble Kew Gardens (from which the writers had come), their luxuriance needing no recourse to hot-houses. Outstanding among them is Anfa which must be one of the most beautiful residential suburbs in the world. It was here that Sir Winston Churchill, President Roosevelt and General de Gaulle met for the Casablanca conference during the war. Photographs of them, with the King and Crown Prince of Morocco, still adorn the walls of some of the prestigious villas where they stayed.

Despite its lack of tourist appeal Casablanca has remained the favourite home of foreigners and Moroccans alike. For the wealthy it offers a sybaritic existence in the sports' clubs, where the cult of excellence is taken seriously, at beach clubs, whose members appear to while away their days endlessly sunbathing, in excellent restaurants (one of which holds the cup for the best restaurant in Africa), and at elegant dinner-parties in luxurious private villas.

The Corniche of Ain Diab is the sanctuary of the high priests of this lotus-eating life. Here are the best fish restaurants; here, throughout the summer, the crowds drift happily from café to ice-cream parlour; the vast public beach at the end of the corniche is black, as though covered with a swarm of giant ants. But it is the unpromisingly rocky shore along the corniche which is the real holy of holies. Here are the exclusive beach clubs and, most exclusive among them, the Sun Beach, the Club des Clubs de Casablanca. Here, wealthy businessmen and *jeunesse dorée* idle away the mid-day hours over appetizing lunches or acquire a yet deeper tan among the jagged rocks. The atmosphere is undiluted, pleasurable ease, enhanced by the beautiful girls and elegant women, Moroccan and French alike, parading in their brief bikinis, and the pampered cherub-faced children romping affectionately around their fathers, before running off to create more havoc beside the pool. Yet here, it is whispered, at least two thirds of the city's business deals are concluded; here politics, economics and high finance are dispatched in discreet conversations among the rocks. Here one can admire the quintessence of Moroccan style.

The other side of Casablanca is the other face of life in Morocco. Overcrowded suburbs, without a blade of green, stretch endlessly towards the bleak countryside. The shanty towns reach their tentacles out beyond the new apartment blocks, or weave in among the houses and factories and cemeteries on the northern side. Here, for many families, life is lived on a shoe-string; there is no security but the generosity of relatives. Blood is thicker than water and the family will provide – provided there is a family to do so. The development of industry and larger enterprises is altering the old patterns of personal employment. This, along with a growth of trade unions and widespread unemployment, is creating a quite different working-class environment in the Casablanca of today.

It is a pity that Casablanca is best known abroad by the film of that name, of which not a scene was shot in Morocco. But perhaps it is not

entirely surprising. For Morocco is, at heart, a secretive land, which takes some time to reveal its hidden self and Casablanca, newest and brashest of its cities, retains, after all, much of the character of Fes, the Souss, Tangier and Tetuan and all the other ancient towns and villages from which it has sucked in its motley population.

Tangier

Tangier is the most 'British' of Moroccan towns if I may use the expression without creating a wrong impression. You will seek in vain there the echoes of Tunbridge Wells which ring through the streets of Gibraltar. The quantities of sterling which flowed from the British treasury into Tangier in the seventeenth century

and which so concerned (and, incidentally, enriched) Samuel Pepys, have left little trace. Yet, over the centuries, it has been Tangier which has alternately fascinated, enticed and disgusted the British with its tantalizingly strategic position, its proximity to Gibraltar, its delectable winter climate, and its exotic Moorishness.

During the twenty-two years when Britain owned Tangier most of her expenditure on the town was military. She built a series of forts to reinforce the great walls, which still enclose the *medina,* and to win control over enough of the hinterland to allow for a little hunting, a bowling green and a few gardens. Above all, the British laboured and spent on the construction of a mole to give a protected anchorage. When

Charles II decided to abandon the town he ordered the destruction of his major work, the mole. This was almost as long and arduous a task as the construction had been. The futility of the British effort was noted in the pained reproof of Sultan Moulay Ismail: 'And as to the Mold which you have destroyed, if you had left it as it was, we would have paid you the price of it. And this would have been beneficiall to yourself . . .' – as a staging post on the route to India.

Since the British were under siege for much of their stay in Tangier they supplied the town from Spain. In later centuries the tables were turned and, when the Spanish closed the frontier with Gibraltar, that garrison was victualled from Tangier. Nelson communicated with the British mission there before the battle of Trafalgar and his letters and treasure-chest were held at the consulate until it closed. Tangier, indeed, became of growing importance to Britain throughout the nineteenth century. The long service of the Drummond Hays, father and son, who served as consuls-general (and eventually minister), won for their country a quite unrivalled influence at the Moroccan court. When, in the early twentieth century, her special position was clearly lost in Morocco, Britain was able to insist that Tangier became an international port to avoid it falling under the control of either France or Spain.

Even today, for the majority of British visitors, Tangier *is* Morocco. More English people visit Tangier than any other Moroccan city, many still live there, the residue of a once-numerous, cultivated, sun-loving British community. Every now and then a splendid British villa, with an idyllic landscaped garden, is offered for sale. In 1980 the beautiful old British consulate-general was finally closed; it marked the end of an era.

Today's visitor will feel nothing of the elegant 'British life abroad' of the last century when the Master of Hounds used to bring his pack across from Gibraltar for a little foxhunting and when

there were 'more tea parties than at any other place of its size that I ever heard of', as Lady Agnes Grove remarked at the turn of the century. Foreigners then were not yet commonplace and the appearance of a westerner could still cause a stir: when Elizabeth Murray was carried shoulder high through the water, from ship to shore, correctly dressed, as she thought, in the style of the 1840s with her hat and gloves, stockings and ribbons, she heard herself described by the local women as 'the Nazarene woman covered with little rags'. Nor will he rediscover the Tangier described by Rom Landau in 1952, the romantic centre of every kind of political intriguing and international trafficking ever heard of, when the Café de Paris (today a rather stuffy tearoom whose illuminated pictures of ice-cream sundaes and fancy gateaux are sadly reflected in the glass stand with its tired caramel custards and ordinary cakes) was the vibrant haunt of foreign spies and agents and exiled Moroccan nationalists.

From the sea Tangier is as beautiful as ever, a pile of white squares and oblongs of houses, packed close within the old brown walls, rising steeply over their little hillside from the golden beach and deep-blue waters of the Mediterranean. It is a town of entrancing vistas, from within as well as from without, the very steepness lending itself to sudden unexpected views through archways and gates, from terraces and from the surrounding hillsides. Enter from one of the lower gates and make your way up steeply sloping, often stepped streets, between white-walled houses, whose wrought-iron window grilles recall those of Andalusia more than of Marrakesh. There is no traffic here and few animals. On the concrete path a group of children have marked out a hopscotch patch and are earnestly pacing it out. At a corner a group of countrywomen have seated themselves against the wall and spread out their salad greens, chickens and eggs for sale.

I asked about an old *medersa* and was courteously shown into a lively primary school whose

Tangier (ONMT)

director insisted that I visit every class. This was the old college, they assured me, converted for use today, though it was like no other old *medersa* I had seen. The older children were studying in French while the little ones were learning to read in Arabic. All greeted us

gravely, apparently not at all surprised or reluctant to have their lessons thus disturbed.

At the highest point of the hill you enter another line of fortifications within the town wall. This is the *kasbah*, the fortress and administrative centre of the old town. The old govern-

106

miles distant across the Straits; small wonder the *medina* feels, even today, so Andalusian. From the opposite side of the square, the Bab al Assa, an arched gateway beside a fine old tiled fountain, leads through the inner rampart and commands an extensive view over the *medina* below. Here, in the past, the punishments ordained by the tribunal were carried out on the spot.

Work your way back to the lower part of the town and you will come to a former market place, the Socco Chico, a narrow square within the *medina,* now surrounded by pavement cafés and, at eventide, full of people. From there, a street lined with shops selling Moroccan crafts and other tourist items leads to the city wall and through the gates to the Socco Grande. Once the town's main market this wide square is now part lawns, part roadways. The market has been banished to the lanes and alleyways leading off the square, but is none the less picturesque for all that. Tangier, more than any other town I can think of (except perhaps Goulimine in the far south-west) is a town to visit on market days, in this case Thursday and Sunday. On those days the country women come in from the Rif and the surrounding hillsides, clutching their squawking chickens, baskets of eggs, bundles of vegetables and other produce. They set up their stalls in the little market lanes or simply settle down on the pavement to sell their goods. They are one of the most colourful sights in the whole country, with their wide-brimmed straw hats with dark-blue cords and pompoms, bright red-and-white-striped skirts (the same striped piece of material may also be worn as a cape over their shoulders), and green- or white- or pink-towelling capes. The older women may wear leather gaiters under their voluminous skirts; all wear several layers of dresses under their uniform stripes. For a day the old town is alive with their vibrant colours; at nightfall they return to the mountains.

The lanes from the Socco Grande lead off to the new town, over the hill of the consuls, where the roads still bear names such as Rue

ment palace, treasury and tribunal are grouped around a sloping cobbled square in the corner of which stands a lone palm tree with, beside it, an archway leading out to a platform above the cliff. Look through the archway and you feel you could almost touch the hills of Spain, a few

d'Angleterre or Rue de Hollande, and down into the vast expanse of modern streets which now quite dwarf the old *medina* and its nineteenth-century suburbs. This new town echoes those of Casablanca and Rabat; it is firmly twentieth-century Moroccan in atmosphere and ambitions. The ghosts of the past have gone – even the active nationalists of yesteryear and their families have removed to Casablanca or Rabat.

Along the Coast

Agadir. The very name evokes sun and sand and sea. Agadir is the resort of today and tomorrow; after Tangier it must have become the best-known place in the land. Yet for amateurs of things Moroccan Agadir must come at the bottom of the list. It is a totally modern town set on a beautiful wide bay; its streets and gardens and copses of umbrella pines are clean and well manicured; its numerous brand-new luxury hotels are quite sufficiently luxurious with their heated swimming-pools and international cuisine; its sports facilities include tennis, riding, swimming, sailing, wind-surfing, and a heady combination of water-skiing and hang-gliding.

The life of the town revolves around a successful, highly modern shopping precinct, cobbled and in raw concrete, with craft shops, boutiques, restaurants and a good local food market. In the neighbouring streets are a choice of cafés with colourful tables and sun umbrellas set on the pavement under jacaranda and pepper trees. Their menus feature lobster, king prawn, *loup de mer* and strawberries nearly all year round. A septuagenarian Englishman, retired and happily resident there, remarks that he never misses his morning and afternoon bathe in the Atlantic; even in mid-January the sun can be so hot that the freshness of the sea is a relief. And yet, the climate is such that it is very little hotter in August than in January – indeed, I have often found the noon heat greater in winter than in summer. Then the air is crystal clear, lacking the haze and sea-mists of summer and the sunlight is of a pure intensity. No doubt this is the place to come to relax in the sun; in this international holiday atmosphere anyone may feel at ease.

For Agadir is a sparkling new mushroom development, born out of the tragedy of the earthquake which, one February night in 1960, destroyed the town in five minutes flat, burying half the population under their homes. To the north of the new town is a hillside, planted now with pine trees, where the stumps of walls and traces of pipes and roadways are all that remain of the town that was. A yet more poignant monument to the past is the *kasbah,* a ring of great walls on the highest point of the hill, closing the bay to the north. Within, all is silent: the stone-strewn hillside marks the site of one of the most densely inhabited districts, totally demolished by the earthquake.

The *kasbah,* in the past, had served as a base for operations against the Portuguese who, in the sixteenth century, held most of the ports along the coast. They had, indeed, held Agadir, which they called Santa Cruz. The Berber name 'Agadir' means a fortified storehouse and was significant in those troubled times.

All along the coast, between Agadir and Tangier, then eastwards by the Mediterranean shore, are delightful old harbours which owe their architectural attraction to those struggles of the past, their fortifications built sometimes by the Portuguese or Spanish to keep out the Moors, at others by Moroccans to keep out the Europeans, yet again by christian captives or renegades for the Sultan of Morocco. Essaouira, the first of these harbours, which you reach travelling north from Agadir, is of the latter type. Its name means 'the little picture' and so it was called by its delighted founder, Sultan Sidi Muhammad. He had ordered a French captive to design and supervise construction of the town to replace the old harbour of Mogador which, for centuries, had been the port for Marrakesh. Thus the walled town we see today was conceived as a whole and built in the mid-eighteenth century. Its straight streets, imposing

grey-stone walls and well-fortified harbour do, indeed, produce an elegant and satisfying whole. In the past century trade with Europe flourished: the botanists from Kew watched bales of esparto grass being loaded on its quays, destined for London and the production of paper on which *The Times* was printed.

The most attractive corner to visit is the Sqala de la Kasbah, the gun platform overlooking the sea. Below the cannons a row of arched

Potter in Safi (ONMT)

110

storerooms, built into the ramparts, provide workshops and shops for highly skilled carpenters who produce beautifully inlaid boxes, tables, bracelets and chests from the roots and branches of the thuya tree. They are one of the most interesting purchases you can make in Morocco. Out to sea, beyond the walls, are the rocky islands which were first inhabited by the Phoenicians, then became the site for the extraction of purple dye from murex shells.

A fresh sea-breeze blows throughout the summer, cooling the air and making Essaouira a welcome refuge from the heat which hits you quite suddenly some twenty kilometres inland. Continue northwards along the coast, however, and you reach another historic and interesting port, Safi. Again, there is the strongly walled *medina,* complete with two imposing Portuguese forts built in the sixteenth century in a vain attempt to secure the town. Safi is, today, quite an industrial centre with its large chemical complex for processing phosphates to the south of the town and the fish factories in the southern suburbs. It is the potteries, however, which climb the hillside just to the north of the old city walls, which attract the visitor. Here, beehive-shaped white kilns, their tops truncated and blackened with the smoke of brushwood fires, are set among the potters' workshops. Bowls, vases and pots of all shapes and sizes are turned out with remarkable speed and skill and painted in a maze of colours and complex patterns. The potters welcome visitors and are happy to demonstrate their skills and pose for photographs for a small tip.

Another drive along a spectacular road, hugging the rocky hilltop, brings you down to the greatest Portuguese fortress of them all, Al Jadida, the Mazagan of European history. This strongly walled little town, with its very European streets, houses and abandoned churches and its heart-shaped bastions, held out for an incredible 250 years of almost constant siege, long after the other Portuguese ports had reverted to their original owners, the Moroc-

cans. Finally, it was peacefully evacuated, as Tangier was by the British, with the ultimate acceptance of the fact that a town, which had been built to trade with the neighbouring countryside and yet which was cut off so completely that its inhabitants scarce dare step outside the walls and for long periods must bring all their water by ship from their homeland, was an expensive liability rather than a profitable investment. The great vaulted Portuguese cistern, at the heart of the main fortress, is a touching reminder of those wasted efforts. It is a particularly beautiful and dramatic building, the stone ceiling supported on rows of fine columns, the distant sunlight filtering through the well-like opening in the roof and reflected in the perennial pool of water on the floor. Here were shot some of the scenes in the Orson Welles' film of *Othello.*

The Portuguese mined the town when they evacuated it. Disgusted by the destruction and the large number of casualties the Moroccans left the place empty and in ruins until, in the early nineteenth century, a Jewish community made their home there and the town was renamed Al Jadida – 'the new place'. Many British Jews from Gibraltar settled there and a thriving merchant community developed. Today, the old town again has a partly deserted air and consists of a strange mixture of ruined Portuguese houses and some fine nineteenth-century merchants' homes.

A splendid old bakery has been built into the thickness of the ramparts, just beside the sea gate. It is the most picturesque place in Morocco to watch traditional bread baking; above, the chimneys exude the smell of fresh bread which pervades the ramparts near the sea.

A few miles north of Al Jadida another ancient walled port stands on the banks of the Oum ar Rabia river. Its white houses drop straight to the waters of the river in a setting which seems made for the landscape artist. This is Azemmour. The Portuguese held this little town also, though briefly, and the atmosphere of its narrow

streets is purely Moroccan. The river estuary, with its sheltered anchorage and supplies of both freshwater and seawater fish, has always been its livelihood. The river had its dangers too, before the bridges were built, when its swollen waters threatened travellers who crossed on little rafts, their animals swimming behind. A folk story is told that, long ago, the evil *jinn* of the river blocked its waters and demanded of Azemmour a tribute of forty young men and maids to release the water again. The people pleaded that they were too small a town to sacrifice their young people like that so the *jinn* agreed to accept forty of the town's elders instead. The matter was discussed and only one old man offered himself. He was sent to try to negotiate with the *jinn,* who, moved by the old man's pleas, finally rolled aside the boulder which held up the waters. But, unknown to the old man, his colleagues had followed him and hidden at a

safe distance to watch; when the waters roared out of the cave, all were swept away. The *jinn* had claimed his tribute. And each year, they say, forty lives are lost somewhere in the Oum ar Rabia and the people of Azemmour shake their heads and know who has claimed them.

Another great river, which could also bar the passage between north and south, is the Oued Loukkos, between Rabat and Tangier. A little inland, on the main river crossing, stands the town of Al Ksar al Kabir ('the great castle'), a fortress, which was once the key to the north. Leo Africanus tells an old story of its founding in the twelfth century by the great Sultan, Yakub al Mansur. The King was lost in a storm and asked a fisherman to ferry him across the marshes to the royal camp. 'I would not take you, even were you the King himself,' the fisherman replied. Yakub asked why, and the fisherman replied that in such a storm he feared

his passenger might drown. 'What is the King's life to you?' the Sultan asked; the fisherman replied that he was grateful for the peace and security established in the land. He lodged and fed his unknown guest and in the morning took him to the camp. When he realized who his guest had been he was afraid but the King was grateful and touched by the fisherman's words. He built a town and walled it strongly and gave it to the fisherman. And thus arose Al Ksar al Kabir.

Ksar al Kabir was the site of many battles over the centuries, but none more famous, nor more crucial to the fate of Morocco, than the Battle of the Three Kings. The Portuguese, in 1578, determined on a great onslaught which might win for them Morocco. Their army was led by their young King, Sebastian I, who was supporting a deposed former sultan of Morocco, Al Mutawakil. They clashed with the Moroccan army, coming from the south, between the Oued Loukkos and its subsidiary, the Oued Makhazin. The Moroccan King, Abd al Malik, was already a dying man as his army approached the enemy, but he demanded that, nonetheless, he be borne into battle in a litter at the head of his troops. His army carried the day but he died before the end of it. Al Mutawakil was killed too and in the defeat the King of Portugal was drowned. The battle sounded the knell of Portuguese ambitions to dominate Morocco, for their young King left no heir and Portugal fell under the rule of the Spanish crown while Morocco gained one of her great rulers, the survivor of the day, Ahmad al Mansur.

At the mouth of the Loukkos stands the attractive walled town of Larache, another desirable harbour, which changed hands several times over the centuries. The narrow lanes within its old walls were protected by two

113

Larache (Jean-Luc Soler)

114

strong fortresses which assured the entrance to the important river mouth. Always a key site the cliffs of Lixus, across on the other side of the river, had been fortified and inhabited by Phoenicians and Romans. There are extensive ruins on the hilltop and they include the only amphitheatre so far found in Morocco. From the temple area, at the very top of the hill, there is a beautiful view of the river winding along the oued below, of the old walls of Larache on the far bank and of the sea beyond.

Just to the south of the river are the remains of the frontier posts of the most recent attempts to divide the country along the river line. Here stand, incongruously on a country road, the abandoned customs buildings of the French and Spanish zones in the days of the Protectorate. A little beyond them, among the trees on an old road, is one of the best of the country inns of Morocco, the Auberge de La Route de France; it is worth arranging your journey to be able to eat there, especially during the game season.

Asilah, most northerly of the little walled ports, is the one which can be most easily visited from Tangier only half an hour's drive away. Its massive brown-stone walls were built by the Portuguese and King Sebastian set out from here to the fatal encounter at the Battle of the Three Kings. The close-packed old town within the walls is Andalusian in character. The narrow lanes admit no traffic; the houses are painted white with green or blue doors and Spanish-style wrought-iron balconies. The people have a love of colour and have painted brilliant murals, geometric patterns for the most part, on the outer walls of some of their houses. The town attracts lovers of music to the summer music festival which, in June and July, gathers leading groups and singers from all over the world. Despite its stormy history, which continued into the present century when it was the stronghold of the brigand chieftain, Raisuli, there is now a bright and cheerful atmosphere about the place and it is surely one of the most appealing of this chain of delightful, old, walled coastal towns.

Harvesting oranges (ONMT)

116

7 Life in the Countryside

The Landscape

Morocco enjoys 'an almost unequalled climate' reported the botanists from Kew who studied the flora in 1871. Whatever else may have changed in Morocco over the past century, the climate remains the same, always sunny, always clement. In summer it is rarely unbearably hot except, of course, in the desert or for a few days at a time in the inland cities, such as Marrakesh and Fes. In winter it is never cold except in the high mountains where snow lies for months on end.

As I write now in Casablanca, in the week before Christmas, the sun streams in through my window. The air is fresh and one puts on a pullover to go outside. The gardens and countryside are green for there was a little rain earlier in the autumn to break the habitual long drought of summer. But the local people are worried. After the first rain the farmers sowed their crops. If it does not rain again soon the new shoots will wither and the vital grain crop will be lost. I have stopped greeting shopkeepers with a cheery, 'Isn't it a lovely day,' for they immediately look glum and reply, 'Ah, but we need rain.' Even in the city concern is real.

Each year, as winter approaches, there is the same anxiety. Throughout most of the great plains of Morocco, and the mountains as well, the crops are rain fed and rain falls only in winter. If the rains come too late the crop may be lost. In the past this meant famine in the land; today, famine can be averted by importing more grain but the burden on the economy is severe. Fortunately, this year it rained copiously in the rich grain-land of the Doukkala to the south; the Casablanca region still waits and hopes.

The autumn rains bring the landscape to life. Shortly after the first rainfall the parched yellow countryside becomes green, the fields fill with wild flowers and the cattle and tall, white egret birds wade through carpets of orange and yellow marigolds, white daisies and narcissi, red poppies, mauve and blue mallows, tall white and pink asphodels, blue iris and magenta gladioli, or under bushes of yellow mimosa, gorse and broom. The country children make elaborate bouquets of wild flowers – tall cones in stripes of different colours – which they sell by the roadside.

The wild flowers are a winter blessing but the trees are a pleasure all the year round. Morocco is still basically a well-wooded country and one variety or another of tree will grow almost to the summits of the Atlas mountains and down into the confines of the Sahara. Very common in mountain and plain are the evergreen oaks – the cork oak and the holm oak – which form the basis of the great forest of Mamora to the north and east of Rabat; it is the largest cork forest in the world. The outer bark of the cork oak can be stripped every ten years, leaving the trunks a deep mahogany red which weathers to black. The inner bark provides tannin, much in demand for the city tanneries, but this must be taken with more care for if the tree is ringed more than half way round it will die.

The thuya or gum sandarac tree is a native of north-west Africa and also very widespread. Its wood is sweet-scented and well suited to cabinet making for it is impenetrable to worm. The wood of both branches and roots is used in the construction of round tables and fine boxes; it is made into rafters and charcoal and the gum is used in the manufacture of varnish. There are pine and fir trees and mighty cedars in the mountains while, in the south, grows the strange argan tree found only in Morocco.

Growing quite differently from these wild trees are the extensive plantations of olives and citrus fruits, laid out in neat rows and clothing the hillsides with their ruler-straight lines. Oranges, lemons and grapefruit hang heavy on the trees throughout the winter and piles of them are sold by the roadside. We picnicked one day beside an orange orchard near Meknes and were disappointed to see people coming from under the trees where we thought there was nobody; they approached us, their arms full of oranges which they desposited at our feet, wishing us *'bon appetit'* before returning to their work in the orchard.

The olive is an ancient cultivation in Morocco as it is all round the Mediterranean. The hills above the Roman city of Volubilis are grey-green with olives as they must have been in Roman times to judge from the many olive presses among the ruins. The fruit is pressed in much the same way today. In a small, dark hut, a donkey turns a large vertical grindstone to crush the olives; the shiny, black crushed fruit is then pressed under a heavy wooden press, often a whole tree trunk moved by wooden screws, and the oil flows out through a runnel into a collection trough. In the highly cultivated farms of the Meknes region the olive trees are young and kempt but, in remoter areas and mountain districts, they often grow to a great old age and their vast trunks are gnarled and twisted. A mountain boy showed us round such a plantation, patting the trees as he passed and detailing how many kilos of fruit each one produced.

The grey-green of the olive trees is echoed in the strange, spiky, prickly plants of the agave and the opuntia which both grow so freely that they look as though they had been part of the landscape for ever. In fact, they came from South America and were introduced to Morocco by the last of the Moorish refugees from Spain.

The agave has large, succulent, almost blue-grey spiky leaves and throws a giant flower spike which, in a matter of a few weeks, shoots up to a height of eight or ten metres and from which yellow-green flower spikes branch out in summer. It is known as the century plant from the erroneous idea that it flowers once in a hundred years and then dies. In fact, it flowers after only ten or fifteen years and then the main plant does, indeed, die. The agave is usually planted as a hedge in Morocco, as is its companion, the opuntia or Barbary fig (also called the prickly pear). This extremely prickly plant, with its flattened green stems, makes a hedge which it is painful to penetrate; it is grown around many little country farmsteads as well as to keep animals out of the cultivations. It produces a fruit rather like a large yellow-green gooseberry which it is disaster for the unskilled to touch for the prickles immediately fill one's skin; the fruits are sold in summer in Moroccan markets where the seller usually opens them to be eaten on the spot.

While Morocco was well favoured with natural forests and many of her older roads were deliberately lined with trees, giving welcome shade, the need to replenish the stock is ever present. In recent times extensive plantations have been made of eucalyptus and pine and these artificial woods provide welcome leisure resorts as well as the timber and woodpulp which the country needs.

In the past the country harboured many wild animals most of which have become extinct as man dominated more and more of the land. Greatest of these were the herds of elephants which browsed on the plain in Roman times and were freely culled by the Romans for the circuses back home. King of Moroccan beasts was the lion, once widespread and found until the beginning of this century in the Middle Atlas and in the forest of Mamora. Jackals, leopards and panthers roamed the countryside and wild boar and apes made their home in the woods. Today apes and wild boar are still found in the

Date palm grove

Water from the mountains

Market of Larache   (Jean Luc Soler)

Fantasia rider   (Gerard del Vecchio)

Threshing

Ploughing in the Rif

Phosphate workings, Khouribga

Rif mountains

Cement factory near Marrakesh

New irrigation channels

Kasbah of Telouet, High Atlas

Our hosts, Middle Atlas

Ouzoud Falls

Berber village, High Atlas

Ait Haddidou woman, spinning

Ait Haddidou girl, Moussem of Imilchil

mountains and there are jackals in remote districts. It is only by a lucky chance that one ever sees the larger wild animals, however, although small animals such as the little grey ground-squirrel may still be glimpsed in the mountains.

The villages in days gone by were close built for protection against both man and beast. In the mountains the *douars* are often perched on a cliff's edge, the walls of each house joined to that of its neighbours to present a continuous outer wall to the hamlet. In the plain, however, where permanent habitations, except for the cities, were less common in the past, isolated farms and widely spread villages are commonplace and show a complete lack of concern for defence.

Security in the plain was provided, if at all, by the occasional fortress or fortified *caravanserai,* known as *kasbahs.* Energetic sultans established and manned lines of such forts. Moulay Ismail constructed several of the most outstanding, among them the great *kasbah* of Kasba Tadla at the foot of the mountains and that of Boulouane, also on the Oum ar Rabia river. Boulouane, between Settat and Al Jadida, is a dramatic example of a royal *kasbah*. It stands on a rocky spur surrounded on three sides by the river and partially separated from the land on the fourth side by a deep gully. Its huge stone walls glow golden in the sunshine. A monumental and ornate gateway on the land side leads into a vast interior court in which are the ruins of a mosque, stores and a high tower. Storks nest in spring on the bastions which reinforce the walls. On the river side a strongly walled walkway drops steeply to the water, protecting access to the river and water supply. A very good local wine known as Gris de Boulouane is produced from the vineyards near the *kasbah*.

A series of *kasbahs,* which many visitors to Morocco must pass, are those which lie along the old coast road between Casablanca and Rabat. They were built not long after the Kasbah of Boulouane to provide secure night lodging places for travellers and caravans going between the two towns. Two or three of them

are today clearly visible from the road and also from the new motorway just inland of them. Each consists of a square-walled enclosure with bastions for extra defence. Today one is incorporated into the military base of Skirat, one has a whole village built inside it and one is simply an empty enclosure, as it must always have been, but littered now with the carcasses of abandoned cars.

Agriculture
The country's most important agricultural regions are in the great plain which stretches along the Atlantic coast and inland for up to 150 kilometres to the foot of the mountains. But this is not the only cultivated ground. The hilly districts around Meknes have some of the most productive farms; the mountains are terraced in steep steps wherever the industrious Berbers could scrape together a little top soil; the southern plain of the Souss valley between the Atlas and the Anti-Atlas and, finally, the oases and river valleys on the fringes of the desert itself, are all diligently cultivated.

While most of the crops are rain fed the people have always made use of small-scale irrigation. The waters of a spring would be led through a winding series of irrigation ditches, known as *seguias,* which fanned out to reach the foot of every olive tree or, finally, to water a whole field. The entrance to the channels was controlled by small dams which would only be opened at a certain time of the day and water rights, determining the amount of time allotted to each farmer, are very complex, though simply operated. A village woman in the Anti-Atlas, for instance, measures the water in a pool with a palm branch marked with two nails. She opens the little dam giving access to her olive grove and waits half an hour or so until the water in the pool has dropped to the level of her second nail. Then she closes the dam, replaces her measuring stick in the crook of a tree and leaves until the next day.

121

The opening of the dams can be quite dramatic. An arid hillside suddenly comes to life with leaping, swirling streams of water as though some giant hand had turned an invisible tap. In a remote Berber village at sunset the steep, narrow, rocky alleys between the houses may suddenly be awash with muddy, bubbling torrents. The village lanes themselves are part of the *seguia* system and for an hour become almost impassable.

Water is sometimes raised to feed the *seguias* by huge, vertical water-wheels called *norias*. These wheels have small buckets around the rim and, as they turn with the force of running water, the buckets fill and are lifted high into the air to empty into the irrigation channel as the wheel turns over. A series of such wheels can be seen on the road between Fes and Khouribga, set against the banks of a small river. Water is also sometimes drawn from wells by means of a wheel turned by a blindfold donkey, mule or camel, walking round and round, but this is more usually for household consumption.

Animals provide the motor power for traditional agriculture, especially in the mountains where the terracing is unsuited to mechanization, and throughout much of the south. Until the turn of this century there was no wheeled transport in Morocco and everything was carried on the backs of animals. Today, one commonly sees donkeys, mules and camels so loaded with crops or brushwood that only their feet are visible, or going to market piled high with pots or baskets stacked above their saddle-bags. The antique wooden plough is pulled by mixed pairs of a mule and camel, a horse and donkey, an ass and an ox and, in the north, by two oxen 'carelessly tied by the horns', as Lancelot Addison described it in 1670.

Mixed teams of animals are also used for threshing, an activity to be seen throughout the countryside in July. Beside each village or even farmstead is a flat circular piece of land on which the cut grain is spread. In the centre is a pole to which the smallest of the animals is tied; the line

Labouring on a mountain terrace

then works outwards in ascending order of size, starting with little donkeys, then a few oxen, then mules, then horses. There may be up to fifteen animals in a threshing team, driven round and round over the cut stems to separate the grain from the chaff.

The people, too, are as closely involved in back-breaking labour as their animals. Women carry home each day large, round-bellied water jars balanced on their shoulder; in the mountains one often meets a line of girls and women bent double under huge loads of brushwood for the fire. In the fields women as well as men bend low to weed the crop and, in June, to cut the grain with hand sickles. On the threshing floor the men run round in circles after the animals to keep them moving and, when the threshing is finished, they toss up the chaff with forks to

123

winnow the grain. Only in September is there some relaxation after the harvest and this is a favourite time for marriages and festivals.

The crops grown vary across the country, according to the climate, but in most regions wheat and barley are by far the most important and the success or failure of the grain crop determines whether there is famine or plenty in the land. Maize, beans and other vegetables are also widely grown, while regional crops include dates in the south and near Marrakesh, almonds in the south, walnuts in the high mountains, melons, oranges and grapes in the plain and olives on the lower slopes.

Hemp is a crop which is also quite common. 'The plant called Hashisha is the African hemp plant; it grows in all the gardens,' wrote James Jackson in 1809. It is frequently smoked by Moroccans as hashish (made from the leaves) or *kif* (made from the flowers and seeds and rather stronger). It is grown extensively in the Rif where the fibres are also used to make mats, cords and baskets. Hashish can be used in cakes and sweetmeats which may be handed round at parties. In *The Alleys of Marrakesh* Peter Mayne describes such a party and the effects of the hashish cakes on the unwary and unsuspecting. 'Si Fulan was beaming at me through the mist that had come up . . . I don't exactly remember the sequence of events – whether perhaps it was now that I danced a slow romantic valse in the costume of a Hussar . . .' The rest of the party faded into oblivion. Hashish can create more trouble for tourists than any other single cause in Morocco for its use is illegal and its purchase, especially in other than very small quantities, fraught with risk. Attempts to export it are also likely to lead to trouble since both Spanish and British authorities are very much on the lookout for this illegal import.

While agriculture is the basis of life in much of the countryside, stock raising is also very important. Everywhere in the country one sees men, women and children standing watching their cows, sheep or goats grazing on land that is unfenced and without hedges. Untended animals hop around, three-legged, near the roadway, their hobbled front legs tied close together. The shepherds in their long, brown *jellabas* give the landscape its tranquil, age-old appearance. In the mountains the shepherd's life is less restful for the tribes must practise transhumance, taking the flocks up to the mountains in summer and bringing them down again in autumn. They live, while away from home, in simple huts or tents or in the fortified communal store houses, and suffer the rigours of sudden change of climate at high altitudes.

Around each farm or village are always flocks of chickens and often turkeys, ducks and geese as well. The wretched chickens are sold by the roadside, lying in the dust, their legs tied tight together or are carted into the towns and country markets to sell.

These country markets are a vital factor of life in the *bled* (as the countryside is called). Across the land many villages and towns have the names of a day of the week, the local market day, often followed by the name of a tribe. The days of the week, except Friday, which is the muslim sabbath, are known by numbers, Sunday being 'One'. So one finds Sebt des Gzoula ('seven' of the Gzoula, a Saturday market), Had Ouled Frej ('one' of the Ouled Frej, a Sunday market), Souk al Arba (Wednesday 'four' market), Sebta (Ceuta – Saturday 'seven'), etc.

Sometimes the markets are in towns and villages but often they are right out in the open countryside, not near any settlement at all. There, in the past, potential enemies might attend the market in peace for it was an inviolate rule that all must go unarmed. Most of these market places were walled during the French Protectorate and many now have imposing arched entrances which look oddly out of place, on non-market days, when they lead simply into an empty enclosure.

On market day, however, the scene is very different for, from the early morning onwards, the country people, mounted on mules or donk-

In a country market

eys or piled onto open flat carts, converge from miles around on the market place. Inside is a scene of intense activity. Tents are set up in lines to serve as booths and here the country produce – fruit, vegetables, handcrafts such as mats, big straw hats, simple pottery, and grain and animals of all kinds – are for sale. At the same time wares from the city or imports occupy a number of stalls – cutlery, scissors, plastic sandals, wellington boots and buckets, leather slippers, cloth and glassware and, of course, sugar, tea, coffee and spices. The latter are sold on the same stall and the country people buy their coffee beans mixed with cinnamon, ginger, sesame, aniseed or peppercorns, which they claim enhance the flavour. A cup of this coffee is quite an experience for the uninitiated; coffee made from beans alone seems insipid to the country people.

The market is enlivened by the presence of animals who help themselves to any unconsi-dered trifles, such as discarded melons and tomatoes and straw hats, or who pursue each other amorously or in spite. The air is rent with the braying of donkeys and bellowing of irate bull camels, blowing out their pink cheek pouches like huge balloons of bubble gum. Sheep purchased at the market may be seen leaving ignominiously bundled into the saddle-bags of a large donkey or mule.

Stalls of one kind are grouped together; the butchers' stalls are always set a little apart for it is feared that blood attracts a host of *jinns*. The markets also provide a tribal meeting place where business can be discussed, marriages arranged, administration of the district carried out. There is often a judge there and, maybe, a doctor, a barber, a blacksmith and a tooth-puller. For the country people, who live in small remote communities, this is the most important social event of the week.

125

It is a far cry from the country markets to the industrialized production methods and mass-marketing of the modern agricultural areas. Across extensive areas of the plain run grey concrete open-topped pipes, often supported on stilts at head level. These pipes carry the waters for important irrigation schemes which feed the expanding cultivations of the Gharb and Doukkala, Tadla and Moulouya. Since the rainfall in the mountains of the Atlas and Rif is considerable and the water runs off to the Atlantic in a number of big rivers, of which the most important are the Oum ar Rabia, the Loukkos and the Sebou, it was seen, long ago, that dams could make a useful contribution to agriculture. Joseph Thompson, a hundred years ago,

described a 'massive dam' above Dimnate. The biggest of Moroccan dams, Bin al Ouidane in the Middle Atlas, was completed in 1955 and feeds the Tadla plain. Over the past dozen years, dam building has been pursued with great energy and the area of irrigated land has been increased by several hundred thousand hectares.

In the areas of new cultivation modern methods of farming are being introduced and tractors and combine harvesters are more frequently seen. The white egret birds seem to appreciate the deeper furrows ploughed by the tractors and flocks of them follow the plough. New crops have been introduced and are of growing importance. Sugar beet is the main one: Morocco, known for its sugar centuries

Sugar factory in the Tadla

ago, had in recent times been importing large quantities of sugar. Now the aim is to make the country self-sufficient in sugar production and many sugar factories and refineries have been constructed in recent years. Emphasis was on the sugar beet but this is now to be supplemented by extensive sugar-cane plantations.

Tomatoes are another crop whose cultivation is increasing greatly and beginning to make use of large rounded greenhouses with polythene covers to produce earlier and better fruit. The tomato was brought to Morocco by refugees from Andalusia where the plant had recently been introduced from South America. Lancelot Addison commented favourably in the seventeenth century on the Moroccan salad 'rarely found in Europe, which they call tomatos'. Today they grow so freely that, in the season, cows and donkeys munch contentedly at piles of abandoned tomatoes.

Strawberries are another exotic plant whose cultivation has been encouraged in recent years. They are now commercially grown in the Agadir region and the season has been so greatly extended that there are only a few months in early autumn when one does not find strawberries in the local market.

Phosphates

While modern agriculture and tree planting enhance the beauty of the countryside no one could say the same of modern mining. Phosphate extraction, on which Morocco's prosperity now so greatly depends, does leave a lunar landscape of mounds and hollows which only grass over when the mine has been abandoned.

Morocco is blessed with the largest known phosphate deposits in the world, estimated at some 75 per cent of world reserves. Phosphates are an essential basis for fertilizers and they account for one third of Morocco's export earnings; a fall or rise in world phosphate prices can be crucial to the country's prosperity. In recent years phosphates have become by far the most important of Morocco's natural resources after agriculture.

The largest and longest established phosphate mines are in the plain around Khouribga. Phosphates are also mined today at Yousoufia near Safi, at an extensive new mining site near Ben Guerir to the north of Marrakesh, and will soon be extracted at Meskala near Essaouira. There are also important phosphate deposits in the Sahara at Bou Craa. The grey, covered wagons of the phosphate trains have become a familiar sight across the countryside and the ports of Casablanca and Safi are largely occupied with shipping phosphates. A considerable chemical industry based on phosphates has been developed at Safi and is being extended. Meanwhile a totally new phosphate port is under construction at Jorf Lasfar near Al Jadida. If you look over the steep cliffs there (Jorf Lasfar means 'yellow cliff') you see the new mole being constructed from grey concrete tetrapods, a kind of modern industrial counterpart to the weird red spider-crabs which the fisherboys brandish for sale along the coast. A phosphate-based chemical complex is to be built at Jorf Lasfar also.

The exploitation of Morocco's phosphate reserves is handled by the Office Cherifien des Phosphates (OCP) which is the country's leading business organization. The OCP was founded in 1920 and now employs some 23,000 people in the production of twenty million tonnes of phosphates a year and the processing of part of this production at the chemical complex of Safi.

Man watering his horse

Girl of the Anti Atlas

Truck 'bus' crossing a ford in Todgha Gorges

Kasbah of Skoura

One of Dra valley *ksour*

Washing in the river, Boumalne

Caravan sign, Zagora

Kasbah of the Ait Benhaddou

8 The High Mountains

The chain of mountains, which form the spine of Morocco and protect her eastern flank, rise ever higher as they run southwards. In the northerly Rif the highest peaks are nearly 2500 metres; in the Middle Atlas they are above 3000 metres and in the High Atlas the Jebel Toubkal is over 4000 metres. This great wall of mountains produces the country's most beautiful and dramatic scenery. Green and well wooded on the slopes facing the sea the vegetation becomes sparse and the rock structures naked and clearly displayed on the inland slopes. And then again, the nature of the woodland and undergrowth changes as you drive upwards towards the high passes or, as you go south, through the different sections of the almost continuous range.

The woodland is largely evergreen but in autumn the Middle Atlas, particularly, is splashed with gold as patches of deciduous trees change colour. From November through to spring snow lies thickly on the high peaks while the lower slopes are already covered with spring flowers long before the snow melts. The Berber villages fit snugly into the folds of the mountainside, climbing high up to the snow line and even above. In the Atlas they are often scarcely visible for they are built of the mud or stone of the region, unobtrusive, close knit and often perched on a cliff for defence. Above the village there may be a fortified storehouse, a *tighremt,* built, perhaps, with four strong corner towers, a place of refuge and security, or a gathering place from which to launch an attack on another tribe.

Life in the mountains was, over the ages, always wild and free. The tribes there were a law unto themselves but, within their own communities, they led a disciplined, democratic existence with no man far outstripping his fellows. The great warlords of the High Atlas are rather a feature of recent times than typical of Berber mountain life. Today, peace reigns in the mountains; the wildness and the freedom too have been curbed but, otherwise, life there continues virtually unchanged. Each village must still be practically self-sufficient, its people dependent on their own skill and strength or that of their animals. Asphalt roads and electricity still reach only a small proportion of them; for the rest, mule tracks, paraffin lamps, water from the stream and the stillness of the mountain valleys must suffice.

The mountain people grow their crops wherever they can scrape together a little soil on a more or less horizontal plane. Pocket-handkerchief fields are cultivated by the bed of a stream, at the turn of a valley or sandwiched between terrace walls. They can only be ploughed by a mule or donkey, and hoed and reaped by hand. Little, jumbled olive groves and lonely stately walnut trees provide much of their sustenance. The women must cope with the daily needs of the household. The provision of fuel and water are major tasks in a mountain area where a touch of a switch does not bring light nor the turn of a tap water. Girls and women must go down to the nearest stream several times a day to fill their large pottery water jars which they carry home on their shoulders or hanging down their backs from a strap over their heads. Firewood usually requires an even longer climb for the land around the village is already stripped of dead wood and kindling and

Bringing in firewood (ONMT)

the girls must go further afield to amass the great bundles, which they pile up on their backs, until they make their way home almost bent double.

In many villages the men are away for much of the year accompanying their flocks to higher pastures in summer or down to the valley in winter. They may live in summer villages of primitive huts on the high slopes or in their black tents of woven goats' hair, held up on a curved wooden yoke supported by two main poles. When they move with their numerous flocks of sheep and goats they risk conflict with the sedentary peasants who are loathe to allow them across the cultivated land. In the high mountains they face snow storms and fierce weather. The independence of their mountain life is dearly bought in terms of toil.

130

The Rif

The Rif mountains drop steeply into the Mediterranean on the northern side then curve inland almost as far as Fes in the south. They are abrupt and were practically inaccessible until very recently when, after independence, the Moroccan government built a number of asphalt roads there. The people are the most fiercely independent of all Moroccan tribes; attempts to pacify them cost the colonial powers dear.

Nevertheless, the Rif has a peaceful, picture-book appearance which could easily have misled the foreigner. The mountain slopes are very green, clothed with cedar trees and evergreen oak above, the valleys below carpeted with wild flowers – marguerites, narcissi and blue iris, the hillsides splashed with yellow gorse and large pink or white rock roses, the river beds lined with pink oleander. From the northern slopes the blue Mediterranean, with its scalloped rocky bays, comes suddenly into view. The hills of Spain are clearly visible across the water. Here and there an old ruined fortress guards an anchorage. Or a little fishing fleet comes into harbour, as at al Hoceima. Soon a quite different monument will mark the coastline – a monument to modern industry in the shape of a huge new steel works to be built at Nador.

The villages and outlying farmsteads have the unexpected look of Irish cabins, whitewashed and with sloping roofs. They were once covered with thatch but, today, only a few thatched barns remain. The houses have all been re-roofed with grey corrugated iron, less picturesque, no doubt, but surely more waterproof. The women complete the picture-book quality of their environment: they wear the red-and-white striped skirts, which we met in Tangier, and wide-brimmed straw hats, often with dark blue pompoms and cords. In their villages many of the children are fair-haired and blue-eyed, a colouring which has always puzzled those interested in the origin of the Berbers and which is only rarely seen in the Atlas tribes.

The mountains are the domain of village life; towns were left to the plains. Yet there is one little town which is truly Rifian and that is Chaouen (or Chechaouen, as it is also called). Chaouen is lodged on the steep western slopes of the Rif where the mountains drop to the plain. Its name means 'the horns', from the peaks above it; its white-painted streets run upwards at a sharp angle, often climbing in broad cobbled steps. It is a charming little town whose terracotta tiled roofs suggest a distant origin and, indeed, it was largely built by muslim refugees from southern Spain. The story is told that, for centuries, these families carefully kept the keys to their homes in Andalusia; perhaps some still do.

In the centre of the old town, beside a great brown fort, is a little tree-lined square where the women sell the attractively-shaped, unglazed simple brown pottery of the north. From the streets above the view sweeps the plain and must have reassured those who used the town as their refuge over the centuries. It proved well-nigh impregnable and in recent wars was only taken when the defenders decided to abandon it.

Chaouen and the Rif mountains were still a stronghold as late as the 1920s when the most heroic chapter in Morocco's struggle for independence was written. The Rifians had never accepted a foreign master and, when the Spanish were granted the protectorate of northern Morocco, they saw their independence threatened. They were led into open rebellion by two highly able and well-educated brothers, Muhammad and M'hamid Abd el Krim, who organized an effective guerrilla war in terrain which was ideally suited to it. Muhammad, the elder and the overall leader, had been editor of a newspaper under the Spaniards, but was imprisoned by them and became disillusioned; his younger brother had studied in Madrid and proved a brilliant commander of their troops. In a series of attacks in 1921 they decimated the Spanish army, which had established a line of advanced posts in the mountains, killing or capturing nearly 19,000, the majority of the Spanish force. The Rifian troops numbered then about 3000. For four years, with their small guerrilla bands, they kept the Spanish army at bay, taking Chaouen and clearing the Spaniards out of the Rif in 1924. They were only finally defeated when the French allied with the Spanish in sending a combined force of 400,000 men, backed by planes, into the Rif. The Abd el Krims were captured in 1926 and exiled, never to return to the Rif. But their name and exploits became the stuff of legends.

To the south of the Rif, and threatened by Abd el Krim's revolt, lay the plain of the Taza gap, with Fes astride its western end. This opening between the Rif mountains to the north and the Middle Atlas to the south, had long provided the corridor linking Morocco with the east. It was always the conqueror's route, the way taken by the Romans, the Arabs, and later by Moroccans conquering eastwards and by dissident dynasties descending on Fes. For the French it had been a line of communication which they could not afford to lose.

The Middle Atlas

The forests of the Middle Atlas grow denser and higher as one nears the top of the mountains. They are at their best above the little holiday resorts of Azrou and Ifrane where, in winter, the snow lies thickly enough to make skiing possible on the slopes of Mischliffen. All around are the forests of evergreen oak, juniper and lofty cedars, whose dark spreading branches tower above all other trees. The forests are the home of the macaque, the tailless Atlas monkey, who may sometimes be glimpsed in chattering troops, swinging from tree to tree. Sadly, their numbers are diminishing rapidly nowadays and baby monkeys are often offered for sale by boys of the neighbourhood, at the roadside.

The twin townships of Ifrane and Azrou, set at the foot of the forest, are fraternal rather than identical. Ifrane is a holiday centre built on European lines; its white chalets, with their slop-ing red roofs, are set wide apart, each in its little garden, like a village in the Alps. Azrou is a far more typical Moroccan town, its flat-roofed houses and shops grouped close together around a central square. There is a lively *co-operative artisanale* here for the people not only specialize in wood carving, for which the materials are so close to hand, but also produce good hand-woven carpets. About a hundred women and girls work at the co-operative, weaving carpets of the local Middle Atlas style, a brown design on a natural-beige wool background. They chatter and laugh as they work, sitting close together along benches in front of their upright looms. Their carpets are sold at fixed, government-controlled prices in the cooperative, along with the objects produced by numbers of other craftsmen working on the same premises. Both Azrou and Ifrane are holiday centres, especially popular in summer when their fresh, cool climate can be a welcome relief from the heat of the plain and the walks and excursions in the forests and surrounding mountains are at their most agreeable.

In summer, the lakes and waterfalls of the Middle Atlas attract townspeople from the plains to sail, water-ski or swim in their cold, fresh waters. Many of the lakes have the strange, perfectly round shape of ancient volcanoes and such, indeed, they often are, for one can see the bubbly, porous brown-black rock of the lava flows scattered over the surrounding hillside. Near Azrou, too, is the source of the great Oum ar Rabia river whose waters spring from the base of a cliff and fall in a beautiful waterfall. Sultans in the past sought to control the crossing of this river, in order to secure peace in their realm, for it often served as a barrier between men of the south and those of the north. The most impressive of such river fortresses is that of Kasba Tadla at the foot of the mountains. The massive golden walls of Moulay Ismail's *kasbah* line the river bank with two fine stone minarets soaring above the ruins of his mosques, stores and barracks within. Even today, it is a home

Washing in a mountain lake

Ford over mountain stream

Bin al Ouidane dam

for army families whose womenfolk sit in convivial groups within the great walls, sorting the grain for their bread.

The abundant water of the Middle Atlas has carved deep into the mountainside, cutting spectacular gorges and, in one place, above Demnate, leaving a natural-stone bridge hung with stalactites. Birds fly to and fro beneath this bridge at Imi n'Ifri and it is hung about with long trailing ferns and lush green plants; the drop into the gorge below is deep and sheer. The place has an antique air which led the local people to fear it was haunted, the abode of *jinns,* to whom they leave offerings in a cave below the bridge. A little way along the cliff the footprints of dinosaurs have been left fossilized in the rock. Some way to the north, above Beni Mellal, the fossilized skeletons of a number of dinosaurs were found on a mountain terrace.

North of Demnate, also, are the Ouzoud Falls, the most spectacular of the natural watercourses in the Middle Atlas. Here a curtain of water falls abruptly over a 100-metre cliff into a deep, luxuriant gorge. The cloud of spray which surrounds the falls is shot through with a permanent rainbow though the sun hardly penetrates into the depths of the gorge below. At the foot of the falls we watched a family of monkeys clambering across the cliff and picking edible plants from a grassy bank. An occasional flash of brilliant turquoise-blue marked the passage of an African roller above them. Along the crest of the cliff, above the waterfall, a line of little huts have been built across the watercourses. They serve as mill houses, the heavy grindstones turning perpetually under the force of the water below, the roar of the falls drowning the millers' voices. Beside the huts the land drops away in a void over which the water leaps.

An hour away to the north is the most impressive of the man-made water resources of the region, the great dam and lake of Bin al Ouidane. The grey dam towers between two hillsides where the valley is at its narrowest; above it, the lake spreads out among the hills and valleys, with hillocks rising above the water as a string of islands. Sailing boats take advantage of this new-found haven, fishermen ply the shores. From the abrupt edge of the mountain range nearby one can see the waters of the dam spreading out over the fertile plain of the Tadla below, through a series of canals and conduits. So steep and high are the mountains here, and so wide the view, that it is like looking out of an aeroplane across the endless farms.

While these well-known sites can now be reached by asphalt road there is no doubt that the mountain tracks offer the most rewarding routes to exploring the Atlas mountains. The tracks have been greatly improved over the years as motor transport has gradually made its way into the remote villages and open-backed trucks run a local bus service. Although a Landrover, Range Rover or similar would be the ideal vehicle for these routes, many of them can be quite safely negotiated in an ordinary car, especially if it has good clearance. The ubiquitous little Renault 4 seems to tackle anything, for that reason. And best still, perhaps, is to leave the car and walk along the donkey tracks, which lead from hamlet to hamlet, in a world where the stranger rarely penetrates. The houses here are square-built of mud or stone, with flat roofs. They have the red-brown colouring of the Atlas itself, with small windows often outlined in white. The people like to live on an open terrace and many houses have an open-air upper room, supported on tree trunks, or the family spend their time on the roof. Both terrace and rooftop are unfenced and little children toddle about there at will, often with a natural cliff adding to the drop below them. But mountain people need a head for heights; perhaps it is wise to learn young.

The people seem to long for colour in their environment: they hang out their red-and-ochre rugs and coverings from their terraces; the women wear brilliantly coloured dresses, one above the other, with the upper layer often gold-embroidered and hitched up to the waist to reveal a different-coloured underskirt; their faces are not veiled but they wrap a red or ochre scarf over their hair and hang coins across their foreheads for festivals. Beneath all this finery they favour green wellington boots or plastic sandals; watch them fording the mountain torrents, driving their hesitant animals before them and you understand why. The men too, if they are not wearing the brown- or white-wool *jellaba* against the cold, often wear a cotton gown in pale blue, turquoise, lime-green or saffron over their warm woollen jacket and trousers. A group of people, in the mountains, is always a delight to see.

We followed a remote track one day, deep into the mountains above Demnate. It was a well-made track, terraced across steep hillsides, cut through rocky outcrops, paved even, in places, where it might have washed away in a storm. True, there were moments of anxiety: streams had to be forded and testing the depth of the water was a cold wet job. We hovered anxiously on the bank: could we cross or not? Such fords can be particularly dangerous in springtime, after the rains or when the snows melt. And then, on a steep slope where the track was cut from the cliffside, we met a truck; but these local truck drivers keep a cool head, they saw us into a little pull-in, then nobly squeezed past on the steep downhill slope.

When we could drive no further we walked for hours along a narrow path in Indian file. Hedges of bramble and honeysuckle grew wild beside the track. In the fields around us the women and children were watching the animals, carding and spinning their wool as they sat and chatted. In a little hamlet a group of women and small children, dressed in the gayest of colours, stood on the flat roof of their farm, watching us. When we waved they beckoned us up to join them and their menfolk invited us into their guest room, a long narrow room painted white and furnished with a cushioned bench around the walls. They served us mint tea from a tall silver teapot in small glasses, then a great platter

135

Our hosts, Middle Atlas

of their walnuts, then home-made bread and a bowl of home-made cheesey white butter in which to dip it, hard-boiled eggs and a spicy vegetable *tagine*. On the wall hung a black cloth banner brought back from Mecca by a relative who had made the pilgrimage. On the floor were local, hand-made wool rugs. After we had eaten tea was served again, a sign that the meal was finished, and we left the hospitable family, regretful that we had nothing to offer them but the biscuits and tinned fruit which were to have been our picnic.

In the heart of the Middle Atlas, near the remote village of Imilchil, is held each year in September the most picturesque of all the Moroccan *moussems,* the Moussem of the Fiancés. It takes five hours or so to drive over the good, but dusty, mountain tracks to this inner fastness of the high mountains. There, in a valley between barren peaks, the mountains come to life; the tribe of the Ait Haddidou collect together to honour their patron holy man, Sidi Oum Ghani, and to marry their sons and daughters. The young people, who spend the rest of the year in remote hamlets or nomad tents, have this one chance to look around and choose a partner to their liking. The *moussem* too, like all others, is the great commercial fair of the year when the animals and produce of the tribe are sold and supplies bought for the com-

ing winter.

The tents fill the valley – large black tents in which to sleep, small white tents which act as stalls, medium-sized brown or white tents which serve as cafés. Lights twinkle at night from far up the hillsides where those accustomed to a semi-nomadic life have pitched their camps in quiet seclusion, away from the crowds. Large open-backed trucks bring in the people from distant villages; many more arrive on mule or horseback. All day long the crowds wander among the stalls, bargaining, buying, selling; at night they are entertained by dancers and musicians of the tribe and by a mobile film show with its own generator.

It is the young girls of the tribe, however, who steal the show. All are dressed alike with a white dress held at the waist with a red, yellow and brown tasselled belt, and over it a black cape, striped with beige, red or blue. Around their necks are the chunky Berber necklaces of amber, coral and silver. They wear a blue-black hood, peaked for girls who have been married before, rounded for those who have not, held in place with coloured bands hung with sequins. Some wear a blue-black veil over the lower part of their face. Others paint their cheeks red with a mixture of carmine and honey and add a few beauty spots to offset the deep-blue tribal tattoo mark which runs down from their lips to their chins. The girls are on the look-out for a likely young husband and they are not in the least shy. Coquettish glances flash from dark eyes; they openly hold hands with the boy who takes their fancy. The conversation soon becomes serious, however: can you cook, can you set up a tent, how many sheep do you have?

When the couple are content that they have found the right partner they go together to the marriage tent where an official registers their marriage. He takes pains to establish the girl's age and rejects numerous candidates whom he finds too small. He also insists that the marriage be her own choice and speaks sharply to fathers who try to answer for their daughters. Many of those who come into the tent wear the peaked caps of married girls. Marriage sits lightly among the Ait Haddidou; if the couple find they have made a mistake they are free to divorce and to come back next year to try again. Many of their marriages, in fact, have been prudently arranged in advance by their parents, anxious to see their daughters married to a cousin to keep the inheritance within the family. But these arranged marriages, too, will often be confirmed at the Moussem of the Fiancés.

Yet the tribe are romantics at heart. They have a Romeo-and-Juliet story linked to two round volcanic lakes, high in the hills above Imilchil. It tells of two lovers, of different sections of the tribe between whom blood had been spilt. The young people knew they could never marry and decided to die together at sunset by drowning. The girl became the lake of Tislit, the boy the lake of Isli. So close together they lie and yet their waters can never meet.

The High Atlas

The peaks rise higher and more forbidding as one travels south into the High Atlas. Most of the time they appear innocuous, their snow-covered crests glistening in the clear sunshine. But they can turn threatening too. One grey day I drove up towards Oukaimeden, the well-developed ski resort bathed in almost permanent sunshine (a haven for shirt-sleeved skiers) high above Marrakesh. As we rose that day, high beyond the villages where the road twists and turns above cliffs which leave you feeling weak at the knees should you look over them, the snow began to fall. Soon it fell like a grey-steel curtain. So long as the car could keep moving all was well. But then the road before us was suddenly filled with sheep, hurrying down from the high pastures to escape the storm. The shepherd, huddled in his *jellaba,* his face shrivelled like a brown walnut and his hair snow-encrusted under his hood, kindly pushed our car to get it going again; but around the next corner came another flock. The journey became a nightmare; for the shepherds and their sheep it must have been purgatory. At least we had the car for shelter; they had no protection from the elements.

In centuries past, before the days of motor vehicles and asphalt roads, the journey over the top of the Atlas in winter could be far more hazardous. Leo Africanus described such a journey which he made in the early 1500s. His caravan left the Tafilalet in late October and became engulfed in snow crossing the pass. The guides fled, but first offered to take him with them, thinking he looked a rich prize. But he was as sharp as they were; he turned aside, pretending

to answer a call of nature, and buried all his gold. When they found no money on him they decided to make the make the best of it and took him with them to seek shelter with some shepherds in a cave. After the storm had passed they found that the whole caravan had perished above them in the snow.

Small wonder that control of the few practicable passes conferred power on the families who could hold them. Greatest of these families in recent times were the Glaoui whose Kasbah of Telouet held the pass near the Tizi n'Tishka. They came to power in the last century when the Sultan's army was blocked near the pass in winter and the Glaoui opted to succour them. Their remote fortress was only occasionally visited by foreigners. Joseph Thompson made his painful way up there in 1888 along paths so steep that the men had to hang on to the tails of their mules to pull themselves up and to act as a brake going down. In the *kasbah* he met, and was most impressed by, a young boy 'who showed an incredible amount of precocious knowledge'; the boy, Thami al Glaoui, was destined to dominate the south of Morocco throughout the first half of this century. But life in the mountain fortress was largely a constant struggle to keep on top of warlike neighbours. When Walter Harris visited the place in 1901 he was begged by the old women to stay on. 'Before you came,' they said, 'no one ever laughed in the Kasba, for the men think only of war, and we women only of death.'

The *kasbah* had not changed by the 1930s and the French, when they managed to build a road over the mountains there, thought it wise to take the more difficult pass over the Tizi n'Tishka, twenty kilometres away. Today, you can easily reach the Kasbah of Telouet, empty and in ruins, by taking a small asphalt road which runs eastwards from the main road over the pass. In the last twenty-five years its mud walls have crumbled and ceilings have fallen in. But the state rooms, with their mosaic tiles and sculpted stucco, are still intact and, from a tradi-

Berber village, High Atlas

tional Berber terrace-room near them, one commands a magnificent view across the Atlas. Read Gavin Maxwell's book *Lords of the High Atlas,* before you go and the *kasbah* will be peopled for you with the ghosts of the past.

The Tizi n'Test, the central route over the High Atlas, is another pass haunted by ghosts of the past. On the banks of the Oued Nfis stands the *kasbah* of the Gundafi, the mountain lords who controlled the pass above, sometime rivals, sometime allies of the Glaoui. Some way further up the pass are the extensive ruins of the fortified mosque of Tinmal, the redoubt of the ascetic Almohads from which, in the twelfth century, they swept down on Marrakesh and went on to conquer the whole country beyond before extending their sway into southern Spain across the Straits. The mountain here is dark and forbidding, it is only thirty-four kilometres below the pass which is the steepest and most impressive of the Atlas routes. The road at the top of the pass itself is not asphalted, though perfectly suitable for cars. From the top the view down over the Souss beyond is breathtaking. The descent on the southern side is breathtaking too. It is a road for those with a head for heights.

These high mountains were unexpectedly well inhabited before the dawn of history and by a people who left a record of their passing in numerous rock-carvings on remote slopes. The easiest place to see these carvings is at Oukaimeden where the hillside, now covered with chalets, was also covered in the Bronze Age with carvings showing people, animals, the strange sun-wheel of the ancient inhabitants and metal daggers. The carvings are scattered among the rocks near the natural rock shelters; the local people will show you some, a careful hunt will reveal others.

Goat climbing an argan tree

The high mountains and valleys below are also the source of a number of valuable minerals – lead, iron, manganese, copper and cobalt are mined there among others. Semi-precious stones, especially amethyst, are prolific and geodes, quartzes and many other attractive rock formations are sold all over the mountains at little wayside stalls. In some villages the enterprising mountain people offer mule treks 'to look for amethysts'.

Below the heights, on the seaward side of the mountains, the vegetation is lush and profuse. Even in the higher valleys deep-purple lavender, pink oleander and the tumbling white flowers of the acacia enliven the juniper-clad hills. From January onwards, when the almond trees burst into flower, there is never a time when one does not find some flower or other in the mountains, from the brambles, violets, honeysuckle and daisies, which recall an English country lane, to the orchids, clematis, geranium and euphorbias which speak of more exotic climes. The scent, of wild herbs, is strong on the hillsides and, of pine trees, in the valleys. The British botanists from Kew who explored the Atlas for plants, a century ago, listed 375 species in one valley, 223 in another. They investigated the curious argan tree which grows over large areas of the western slopes of the Atlas, the Souss, and the Anti-Atlas and nowhere else in the world. Its branches spring low from the trunk and it is largely known to foreigners as the tree hung with goats, for these intrepid animals climb high to browse the upper shoots. Its bark is scaly, like the hide of a crocodile, and its small yellow fruit is bitter though the oil extracted from it is appreciated by the local people.

The valleys in the heart of the mountains are particularly beautiful and some of the loveliest, the Ourika and Ouirgane, are supplied with comfortable hotels (the Ourika in the former, the Roseraie in the latter). For a good French *auberge* meal in the Ouirgane try the Sanglier Qui Fume, especially in the evenings when the coach crowds have gone. These valleys are an enchantment at night, when the day-time trippers have left, and they are still, dark and silent except for the persistent croaking of frogs. There is, as yet, no electricity and pools of light are shed by the paraffin lamps hanging in open village shops where the local people gather to chat through the evening. Elsewhere is pitch dark, lit only by the stars and punctuated by the occasional tiny, green lights of a glow-worm. By day you should visit the village pottery in the Ourika valley. In the dark huts on the hillside above the colourful, well-stocked stalls, the potters sit making the unglazed water jars and the great, brown *tagine* dishes which are stacked by the roadside below.

The mountain people can be amazingly generous and hospitable. We camped once near the Cascades d'Imouzer in the western Atlas. We had planned to eat *couscous,* and to ask the village people to cook it for us, but had not counted on the Eid al Kabir falling on that day. The people would lend us their cooking pots but were too busy with their own festival to cook for us; tomorrow? they offered hopefully. But we must eat, so we tried over our exiguous camp fire to achieve the long steaming necessary. It was then that we learnt how difficult it is to find firewood anywhere near a village. In despair we finally boiled the grain, producing an unappetizingly glutinous mess. At that moment two villagers arrived, attracted by the smell of cooking. Too ashamed to offer them our disastrous *couscous* we gave them cigarettes instead. Next day we hired donkeys and mules in the village for a trek over the hills to a further valley. A village man recognized one of our party and invited us to lunch at his house, all sixteen of us. We were given a sumptuous feast of highly successful *couscous,* followed by the best *tagine* we had ever tasted and then (when we could really eat no more), dishes of *kebabs* followed by fresh fruit. We left the little house, happy and replete; all the honours, we felt, had gone to the Berber villagers on that occasion.

Women of the oasis (ONMT)

142

9 Beyond the Atlas

The western and northern face of the Atlas, which looks to the sea and rises from the fertile plain, is green and welcoming. Its valleys are lush and bright with flowers, even the higher slopes are dotted with juniper, lavender and other hardy plants. But, as one crosses the high passes, the landscape changes abruptly; the southern slopes look out over the desert and the landscape below is tawny and barren, vegetation on the mountainside is increasingly sparse.

East of the Atlas lies an arid landscape which extends to the frontier with Algeria and can be reached through a gap in the Middle Atlas, passing by Midelt. To the south there are three roads of which two cross the high passes of the Tizi n'Tishka and the Tizi n'Test while the third, and most recent, 'the new road' as the local people call it, takes a more gentle route over a lower spur of the mountains between Chichaoua and Agadir. It is the easiest, fastest and best of these roads and the only one which gives no impression of dramatic change for here the southern slopes are clothed in argan trees and the road runs down into the fertile valley of the Souss. On the other roads, and especially that of the Tizi n'Tishka, it is the dry warm air of the desert which blows in your face as you cross the pass; as the road drops steeply downwards the Sahara seems to be coming to meet you.

The Desert

This desert land beyond the mountains was always extremely important to Morocco, an extension, as it were, of the cultivated, civilized areas of the Bled al Makhzen, a source of wealth – and of danger. From the times of the earliest Arab kingdom in Morocco caravans of loaded camels set out across the desert to trade with the negro tribes to the south of the sands and bring back gold. The route was appallingly hazardous but the rewards were great. The merchants of Fes and Marrakesh would wait until hundreds, even thousands, of camels and men had gathered together before setting out. The journey from Fes to Timbuctoo would take about 130 days, Jackson recorded two centuries ago, and the tracks across the desert were littered with the bones of men and animals who had failed to reach the other side. He told of a disaster which had happened just before he wrote his book: in 1805 a caravan, which set out from Timbuctoo for the Tafilalet, found the desert wells were dry; 2000 men and 1800 camels perished from thirst on that journey.

Yet Timbuctoo remained the Eldorado, beckoning the Sultans of Morocco. Ahmad al Mansur, greatest of the Saadian kings and the sole royal survivor of the Battle of the Three Kings, sent a military expedition to take Timbuctoo in 1591. His troops successfully crossed the desert and took the town, but the following year the Sultan died and his army were left abandoned on the other side of the Sahara. A century later the powerful Sultan Moulay Ismail kept a garrison in Timbuctoo to collect tribute but, after his death, they too were left there and married into the local population.

Recently, the Sahara to the south of Morocco was governed by Spain. In 1975 King Hassan brilliantly seized the opportunity of General Franco's prolonged illness and death to send an

143

Transport in Tafraoute (ONMT)

'army' of unarmed civilians into the Sahara to annex the territory for Morocco. The manoeuvre was a complete success: the Spanish Sahara was shared between Morocco and Mauretania and the Moroccan people were united in their euphoria at the victory and their support for the King. Unhappily for Morocco the Sahara has not proved the unmixed blessing which she expected: local tribesmen, supported by Algeria, formed the Polisario Front which has launched guerrilla attacks on Moroccan bases and townships and has led the country into a costly war to hold both the Moroccan and the Mauretanian sectors of the desert. The addition of the Sahara to Moroccan territory greatly altered the country's outline: Agadir, which

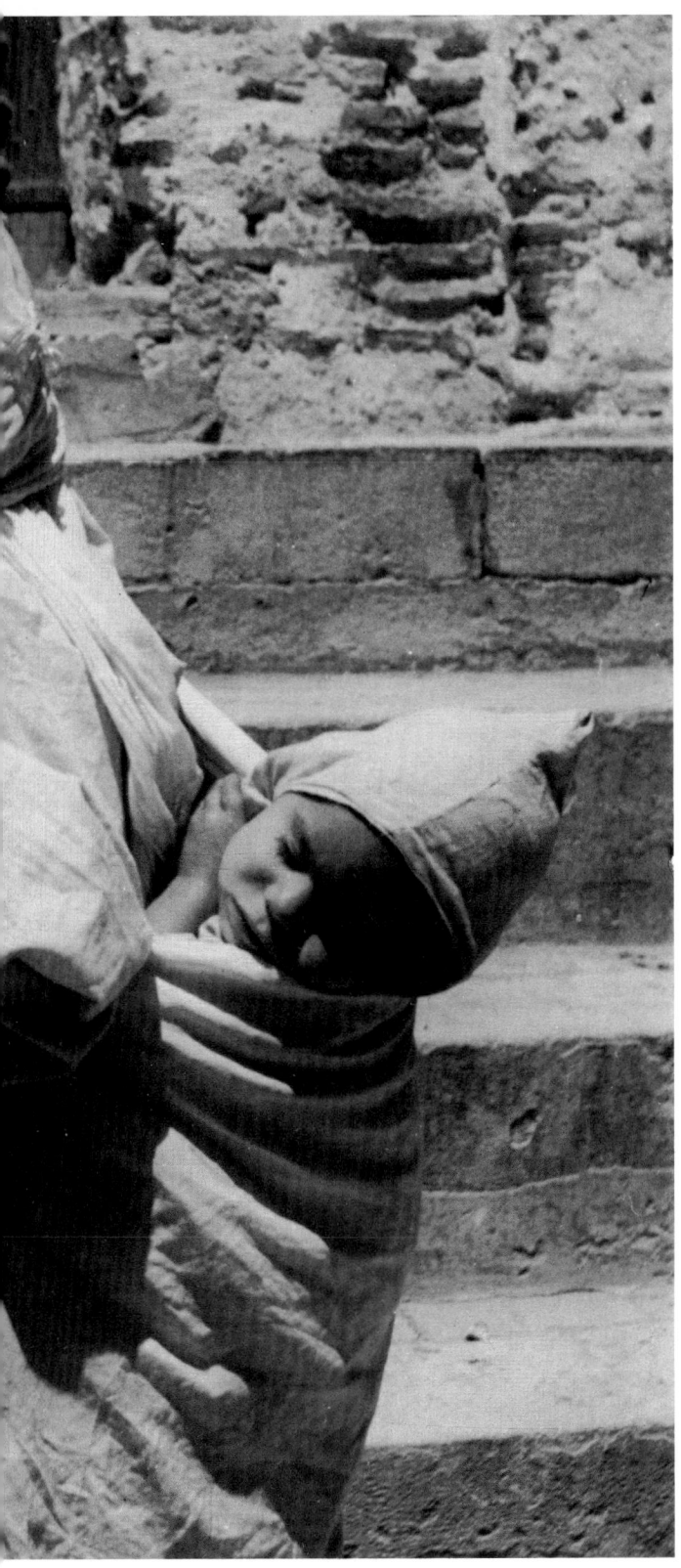

remote that very few of the intrepid travellers of past centuries ever reached it, has been considerably developed in recent times. All the little towns have a French-built town centre with arcaded shop fronts enclosing a central square. A network of asphalt roads runs between the oases and is being extended continually (routes described as 'difficult track' in the guide books may well be good asphalt roads today), and a chain of fine hotels, the Grands Hotels du Sud, ensure a comfortable stay. The most recent of these hotels are superbly designed with simple, elegant rooms. Non-residents may use their welcoming swimming-pools for a small fee.

The Souss and Anti-Atlas
Between the Atlas and the Anti-Atlas mountains the wide fertile valley of the Souss runs down to the sea near Agadir. It has always been extensively cultivated in centuries past, especially with sugar cane and, where crops are not growing, the land is dotted with argan trees on which goats and camels browse. Its people wear the deep-blue clothes of the desert, a long cotton gown for the men, a long, enveloping cotton shawl for the women. The sun always shines: 'There is not, perhaps, a finer climate in the world than that of Suse,' wrote James Jackson and it is this climate which the resorts of Agadir and Taroudant have so happily exploited.

Taroudant is the great capital of the Souss and once, briefly, capital of the whole country. It is an ancient, strongly walled town which, alone perhaps of Moroccan cities, has not developed a new town outside its walls. It stands in total contrast to the new town of Agadir and holiday-makers staying at the latter should at least make the short journey by coach, the long trip back in time. In the centre of the town the little alleys of the *souq* burrow back from near the square. There are some excellent jewellery stalls here, selling the chunky necklaces and heavy bracelets of the Sahara. Stay a while to watch the desert women bringing in their own jewellery to sell to the shopkeepers, going from

used to be considered a town of the deep south, now lies slightly to the north of centre.

There is, however, an important tract of land between the Atlas mountains and the Sahara desert, a land of ancient oasis towns and fertile river valleys which were the homeland of all Morocco's ruling dynasties from the eleventh century onward. This fascinating region, so

stall to stall to get the best price. There is also a modern craft of carving a soft white stone from which the local craftsmen produce some witty little animals and wall-plaques. The lovely courtyards of the ancient Palais Salaam Hotel offer a welcome rest in the shade and a cool drink beside an attractive swimming-pool set at the very foot of the old russet ramparts.

To the south of Taroudant lies the chain of the Anti-Atlas, every bit as beautiful as the mountain ranges further north. Here the valleys and lower slopes are green with the vegetation of the Atlas, while the peaks rise a rugged, barren red-brown wall above particularly pretty villages. In January and early February the valleys are white with almond blossom and the brown-stone villages, with their new pink- or white-plastered houses, are seen through a mist of pink-and-white flowers.

These villages are more decorative, less defensive, than those of the great Atlas chain. Many of the houses have an intricate ornate panel of perforated stone-work rising from the front door to the roof; the doors themselves are often carved. The women wear a black shawl over a long black robe, swathed like a sari and embroidered with a brightly coloured band along the lower edge. They carry fine copper water-jugs to the well or stream, jugs made from copper mined in the mountains. In one village we met a very old man, a Jew aged eighty, who lived alone among his muslim neighbours. He had been sent there for his health a long time ago and the climate had suited him so well that he had stayed on. His little garden was filled with a mixture of flowers, old pots, a ram's horns and a donkey's skull – the same talismans which his neighbours also used against the Evil Eye.

At the heart of the Anti-Atlas lies the little town of Tafraoute, not of great beauty itself, but set in a spectacular bowl of strange wind-eroded rocks which pile up in fantastic shapes all around. It is a good centre for short excursions to a host of neighbouring villages, each prettier than the next. This is one of the few places

where modern village houses actually enhance the appearance of the old villages, their mauve, pink or white colours setting off the deep-brown stonework of the traditional homes. Here, too, the combination of tall palm trees, almond blossom and sculpted rocks, create a landscape made for the painter or photographer.

Beyond the Anti-Atlas, at the very threshold of the desert, is the little town of Goulimine, the most southerly town in Morocco which one can conveniently visit. Its Saturday market once drew in crowds of the 'blue men', the Tuareg of the Sahara, with their herds of camels. Now it attracts more tourists than Tuareg but it is still an easy place to see an animal market (although a far bigger and better one can be seen at Settat, an hour away from Casablanca), and there are nomad tents scattered over the plain around the town. The little arcaded squares and streets of the town come alive also for the Saturday market. Street traders spread their wares on the ground and tiny alleys house the most antique-looking local *souq* that I have seen. The women of the town are delightfully dressed in bright-coloured robes which cover them from head to foot; there is no inconspicuous black or white for them – they are flamboyant in purple, green, pink, orange or blue. Their gowns are held high on their heads by a little wire fastening like an Andalusian head comb and, tied in a corner of the cloth hanging by their cheek, they carefully carry the key to their door.

The Dra Valley
The road along the Dra valley on the eastern side of the Anti-Atlas also penetrates to the south and is one of the most attractive roads in Morocco. It leaves Ouarzazate to cross the high, barren, striated mountains of the Jebel Sargho, giving you the premature impression that you are already in the great desert. But, on the further side of the mountains, you drop down into the little market town of Agdz, its central square lined with jewellery stalls, a regular Aladdin's cave of

146

Berber jewellery from the tribes of the desert mixed haphazardly with modern products from the craftsmen of the towns.

Beyond Agdz you enter the private world of the Dra valley, a desert land where a river actually runs (before disappearing for ever under the sands), where palm groves grow along its banks for 100 kilometres or so and where the fortified mud villages, *ksour,* of the local people testify to their need for self-sufficiency. This is the heartland of the Berber *kasbahs,* the region where, at every turn, one sees decorative family fortresses carefully built of mud and chopped straw with towers and crenellated battlements, or fortified villages, *ksour,* with equally decorative towers and entrance gateways. The Dra valley, too, is the only region where the *ksour* are kept in a perfect state of repair, where their walls are smooth and kempt, their decoration as clear-cut as the day it was made. Elsewhere in the south the *kasbahs* look like sand-castles over which the rising tide has begun to wash; here they are pristine, defying the waves (or, in their case, an occasional torrential shower of rain).

The *kasbahs* of southern Morocco are an interesting architectural puzzle. They have recognizable features of so many diverse origins: the tapering towers of the Arab east, the lay-out of a Roman *castellum,* the mud-brick decoration of ancient Mesopotamia. They are a complete contrast, too, to the discreet Arab town houses of the north with their plain exteriors and luxurious inner courtyards and living-rooms. These *kasbahs* show their finest face to the world; inside, the rooms are plain, higgledy-piggledy, squalid and largely unfurnished. There are no fine painted ceilings or tiled floors. Animals and men share the same abode (the animals below and men above) at night; by day, a low round table and a mat suffice for those who stay indoors.

Zagora is the main township of the valley where you will find a Grand Hotel with a welcoming swimming-pool as well as a smaller

Dra valley

147

Mud-built *kasbah* (ONMT)

hotel and a nice tree-lined camping site. From the ruins of an ancient fort, on a steep hillside above the town, you can look back along the valley with its waving palms and on to the sand dunes of the desert beyond where nomads will invite you into their tent for mint tea. Out there the desert scenes of the film of *Lawrence of Arabia* were taken. From there, also, came the dynamic dynasty of the Saadians who, more than anyone else, were responsible for pushing the Portuguese out of Morocco.

In the centre of Zagora stands a gaudily painted road-sign with a picture of camels and an arrow pointing southwards with the hopeful instruction: Timbuctoo fifty-two days. Jackson, in the days of caravans, had estimated fifty-four

days' travelling time and as much again for rest halts. But, today, the deserts are crossed by trucks and there is a little airstrip at Zagora.

The asphalt road continues now for twenty-two kilometres beyond Zagora to Tamgrout where a collection of medieval manuscripts has been preserved in a religious settlement. They include illuminated Korans written on gazelle skins.

Oases and Gorges

Ouarzazate – how romantic a name for so prosaic a place. At the foot of the great Tizi n'Tishka pass, and at the gates of the desert, a great mud-built stronghold would, somehow, be more appropriate than this little modern town strung along a single main street. Yet it is worth stopping here a while to lodge in comfort and look around. There are three good hotels: the Grand Hotel, the Zat and the Club Mediterranée. For some years the Grand Hotel also ran an annex in the ancient *kasbah* of Tiffoultoute, just outside the town in what must have been Morocco's most romantic lodging place, but, with the opening of the other hotels, the *kasbah*, alas, has closed.

In the centre of the town a cooperative displays the carpets of the region, mostly of mustard hues. On the eastern edge is the great Glaoui *kasbah* of Taourirt; you can visit some of its rooms but they are quite plain and rather small, devoid of the decorative elegance of those of Telouet. Beyond this *kasbah* you come, quite unexpectedly in this desert setting, on a vast lake. At least, in years when it has rained, there is a vast lake for its waters are retained by a recently built dam.

A short journey to the north brings you to a perfect example of the sort of place which, in your imagination perhaps, Ouarzazate should have been. This is the village of Ait Benhaddou, fifteen kilometres east of the main road to the pass. The village is a huddle of high, brown-mud *kasbahs*, grouped at the foot of a steep hill crowned with the ruins of a fort. A shallow river runs at the foot of the buildings through a valley lined with tall green reeds. Narrow lanes twist and turn between the *kasbahs*, and on their towers storks have built their nests. Below the *kasbahs*, on the river bank, an imposing crenellated wall and arched entrance-way close in the village. Odd that the gateway should lead incongruously into a ploughed field; it is just the kind of entrance which such a village ought to have, yet clearly it does not appeal to the local

149

Safiya and her baby brother

people. It was built, we are told, for a biblical film made there in recent times. A flimsy reed fence now closes its gateway.

As we climbed the steep alleys towards the fort we passed a small *kasbah* home with two mud towers. A woman sat spinning on a terrace between the towers. When we reached the wall of the fort above a storm, which had been threatening, suddenly broke and we huddled under the broken walls, miserable and indignant to be so wet and shivering in the desert in May. The woman, seeing our plight, beckoned us to her home and sent out her little children, Fatima

and Abdullah, to bring us in. The children, aged no more than eight and six, spoke French, which they said they had learned from tourists, and showed us around their home with the expertise of professional guides and an appealing pride in their possessions: they pointed out a huge grindstone just inside the door, a round mud oven in a little dark passage, a donkey and some sheep in one yard, a family of rabbits and a few chickens in another. Abdullah caught a rabbit and a chicken for our children to hold. Then they brought us into their living-room, high up in the tower, where we sat on rugs on the floor

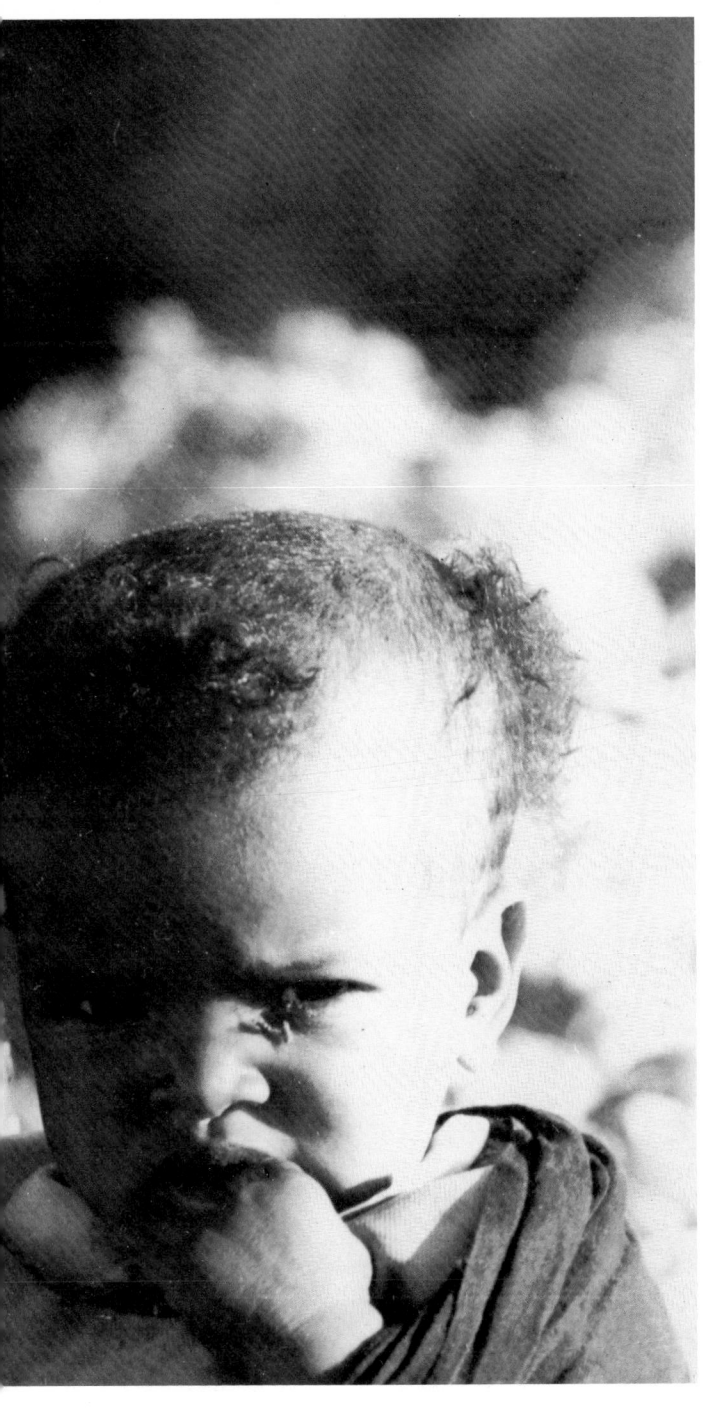

Fatima's age, and just as professional in her approach to tourists, in the village of Kalaa des M'gouna. Her name was Safiya and she came wandering around the Grand Hotel early in the morning, dressed in a brightly coloured gown and carrying her baby brother on her back. The hotel staff chased her away but she sat down on the edge of the cliff to play with the baby, swinging him out over the void to the great amusement of both. She was quite happy to pose for photos and to talk about herself. When I gave her a coin she lifted the skirt of her outer dress and placed it carefully beside the others, hidden away in a zipped-up pocket of her under-skirt.

Take the road from Ouarzazate to Kalaa des M'gouna in early summer and you will be amazed at the delicious scent which reaches your nostrils in the oasis of Skoura and in Kalaa itself. Here pink Persian roses grow in profusion, forming hedges between the fields or planted out in rows. So well do they grow that a rose factory has been built at Kalaa des M'gouna (looking, of course, like a mock *kasbah*) to distil rose essence. The factory was designed in Grasse and produces some of the best rose essence in the world. A festival of roses is held here in May.

From Kalaa to Boumaln the Dades river runs between steep cliffs crowned with *ksour* and *kasbahs*, many partly in ruins and rebuilt above or below the old village. They glow, rose-coloured, in the evening and early morning light, above the blue waters of the river with its fringe of green reeds. The local women, coming down to the water wrapped in their midnight-blue shawls, seem dressed to suit their environment. Only their headscarves, fringed with silver sequins, belong to another world. In Boumaln, itself, a dramatic building on a cliff has this other-worldly mixture of ancient and modern. From a distance it looks like the greatest of the *kasbahs*, its mud-coloured towers piled in profusion. Approach and you find that only the colour is of mud; inside you face the glass wall of the swimming-pool within which the

while their mother made us mint tea and offered biscuits. Their father lay propped up on some cushions beside the window commanding a magnificent view over the other *kasbahs* and down the valley. He took little part in the conversation when his tired-looking wife, with a baby on her back, and her little children tried to entertain us in their halting French and mountain Arabic. When we left we gave the children such small coins as we had; soon after, we saw their father setting off cheerfully towards the village shop.

On another occasion I met a little girl of about

151

Kasbah in Dades gorge

bathers glide like fish in an aquarium. It is the modern Grand Hotel Moudayeq.

Beyond Boumaln the Dades cuts its way out of the mountains through a deep gorge which narrows as you penetrate further into the hillside. The road eventually becomes a stony track. This gorge and the parallel gorge of the Todgha, a little further east, are two of the most beautiful places in the south. Red rocky cliffs rise up to 300 metres high above the perennial streams, little fields by the waterside are intensively cultivated or densely planted with date palms, the ruins of many *kasbahs* crown the knolls or sit astride river crossings. The road itself crosses and recrosses the water, passing great rounded fingers of rock pointing skywards in the upper reaches of the Dades, or plunging into a dramatic canyon in the upper reaches of the Todgha.

152

Further east still, a third river gorge, that of the Ziz, sweeps round behind the Atlas, following the foot of the mountains for many miles. The road here takes a less spectacular route along the cliff-top beside the gorge, instead of down by the water at its foot, but the gorge itself is just as colourful as the other two if you take the time to follow one of the numerous little tracks which drop down into it. Best known of the sites here are the Blue Springs of Meski, where a camping site has been organized in a charmingly wooded grove, where fresh springs burst from the cliff-face. But the site shows signs of too many visitors – litter, boys wanting to be your guide, even a double-decker bus out from London; the less frequented tracks will take you into a timeless world unknown to outsiders.

An asphalt road now runs from Tinerhir, where the Todgha gorge emerges from the mountains, across to Erfoud in the Tafilalet. It threads its way past a string of oases whose livelihood depends on the date palm and where, in autumn, the women and children gather outside the villages to strip the dates from their stems. The discarded orange-gold stem sprays are piled into little fences to mark off the sorting plots of each family; the women and children work within their own patch while the men load the dates into donkey paniers and cart them off to the markets of the Tafilalet where they are sold by the basketful.

A lunar landscape runs between the villages – an area of barren stony desert pockmarked by hundreds of well-like shafts, sunk into the ground, each one surrounded by a mound of earth like the lip of a crater. These are the repair shafts of the *foggaras,* the underground canals, which bring water from the mountains to the cultivation of the plain. They may run for many miles; here the channels run close together, fanning out across the desert. Most of them have fallen now into disrepair and their shafts are blocked with fallen earth. Beyond them, some of the palm groves are dying, others are fed from deeper wells with pumped water. Each of the villages here has its own private character and its women wear their own style of dress. In many villages the women wear colourful clothes and go unveiled but in one village among the *foggaras* the women we saw were all covered from head to foot with a black veil which left only one eye uncovered, reminiscent of the women's clothing in nearby Algeria.

In October a date festival is held in the little red-walled town of Erfoud, main town of the Tafilalet. At that time dates are piled high in the *souq,* seats are arranged around the arcaded town square for the official ceremonies and entertainments and excursions are organized into the desert for visitors. Erfoud is one of the most interesting centres from which to make short desert trips. Beyond the town, towards Mer-

zuga, dunes of pure golden sand rise up to 150 metres high. Nearby, a strange rock layer consists almost entirely of perfectly preserved fossil shellfish. These fossils date back to some 360 million years ago when the Sahara was under the sea. The ammonites, orthoceras and attractive little wide-eyed trilobites were buried in sedimentary layers which here extend for over 100 kilometres towards Zagora. So strange is this shell-filled rock that it seems to have attracted the early inhabitants of the region: fragments of many beautifully polished, green Neolithic handaxes have been found lying above the fossils and local boys occasionally sell complete ones. Today, the fossils exert an even wider appeal: the rock is quarried, sliced into thin slabs and highly polished to produce table-tops, ash-trays, bread-boards and decorative wall-plaques, with their distinctive pattern of curling, round fossils and elongated rocket-shaped ones. The slabs are worked in the big cities and can be bought in Agadir and Casablanca more readily than in Erfoud.

The asphalt road continues south from Erfoud to the little market town of Rissani near Morocco's south-eastern boundary. Beside the town lies a hillside covered with the remains of broken mud-brick walls; it is the site of the ancient and legendary city of Sijilmassa. In the days of the early Arab kingdom of Morocco Sijilmassa was one of the most important cities, perhaps the most important, in the land. On the edge of the desert it controlled the caravan trade to Timbuctoo and hence the source of gold. In the eleventh century the Berber tribes of the desert to the south captured the city and used it as their base from which to conquer the whole of Morocco and to establish their great medieval Almoravid dynasty.

Sijilmassa itself fell into decay in later centuries but was replaced by Rissani with its strongly defensive *ksour.* The lanes in the old part of the town run like tunnels through the buildings. Beside the arcaded town square is an interesting market where women spread out

154

local silver jewellery on the ground at their feet and men make huge baskets or sell large white pots.

Another whole section of the market is devoted to dates, while vegetables and fruit are piled up in pyramids and offered in profusion.

In the oasis around the town are groups of *kasbahs* and *ksour* of substantial construction. Many of them belong to the Alawi royal family whose ancestors came from here. In past centuries sultans sent superfluous members of their family back to the Tafilalet to remove the pres-

sure of too many ambitious sons and nephews in the capital. At home in the ancestral oasis they were suitably housed. James Jackson recorded that a Sultan, in the eighteenth century, brought marble pillars from distant Volubilis to decorate his palace.

It is over 300 years now since Moulay Rashid, the founder of the Alawi dynasty, left the Tafilalet to conquer the key cities of Fes, Taza and Marrakesh in the north. Morocco has come a very long way in that time, from a war-torn feudal state to the pleasant and peaceful

Country musicians (ONMT)

twentieth-century land that it is today. But in the remote Tafilalet, cradle of two of her ruling dynasties, one can still feel the ancient forces which underlay that development. Its *kasbahs* and *ksour* illustrate the need for defence against outsiders; the date palms of the oasis show the struggle to grow sufficient food and to manage available water supplies. In the market place imported goods recall the urge to trade with distant places although, today, there are no longer glittering piles of gold nor dark-skinned slaves. Finally, the mosques and royal mausoleum evoke the importance of Islam in this its most westerly outpost; religion was the spur which drove the conquering tribes of the desert to overrun the lax and indulgent north and establish there, each in their turn, a strongly Islamic state.

Bibliography

In the past many English people have lived in Morocco or travelled there and written about the country. The following is a list of just a few of these books, from which I have taken quotations, impressions or illustrations. It is not in any way a representative bibliography of the country.

Addison, Lancelot, *West Barbary, or A Short Narrative of the Revolutions of the Kingdoms of Fez and Morocco*, 1671

Africanus, Leo, *The History and Description of Africa*, originally published in Italian, 1526; English edition, 1600 (A much-travelled and cosmopolitan Moroccan writer)

Boyde, Henry, *Several Voyages to Barabary. . . the Manner of Redeeming Christian Slaves*, 1736

Drummond Hay, John, *Western Barbary*, 1844

Grove, Lady Agnes, *Seventy One Days Camping In Morocco*, 1902

Harris, Walter, *Morocco That Was*, 1921

Hooker, Joseph & Ball, John, *Journal of a Tour in Marocco and the Great Atlas*, 1878

Jackson, James, *An Account of the Empire of Marocco and the District of Suse*, 1809

Landau, Rom, *Portrait of Tangier*, 1952

Leared, Arthur, *Morocco and the Moors*, 1876

Maxwell, Gavin, *Lords of the High Atlas*, 1966

Mayne, Peter, *The Alleys of Marrakesh*, 1956

Murray, Elizabeth, *Sixteen Years of an Artist's Life in Morocco, Spain and the Canary Islands*, 1859

Ockley, Simon, *An Account of South West Barbary*, 1713

Pellow, Thomas, *The History of the Long Captivity and Adventure of Thomas Pellow in South Barbary* (1720–1736)

Shereefa of Wazan, Emily, *My Life Story*, 1912

Thompson, Joseph, *Travels in the Atlas and Southern Morocco*, 1889

Turnbull, Patrick, *Black Barbary*, 1938

Windus, John, *A Journey to Mequinez . . . in the Year 1721*, 1725

145,00